Critical Guides to Spanish Texts

25 Espronceda: El estudiante de Salamanca

Critical Guides to Spanish Texts

EDITED BY J. E. VAREY AND A. D. DEYERMOND

ESPRONCEDA

El estudiante de Salamanca

Margaret A. Rees

Senior Lecturer in Spanish,
Trinity and All Saints' Colleges, Leeds

Grant & Cutler Ltd *in association with*
Tamesis Books Ltd 1979

ISBN 0 7293 0074 9

I.S.B.N. 84-499-3140-1
DEPÓSITO LEGAL: V. 2.419 - 1979

Printed in Spain by
Artes Gráficas Soler, S.A., Valencia
for
GRANT AND CUTLER LTD
11, BUCKINGHAM STREET, LONDON, W.C.2

Contents

Preface   7

1   Introduction   9

2   Espronceda the descriptive artist   17

3   Dramatis personae   33

4   The narrative. Sources and structure   59

5   Conclusion   69

Appendix: Espronceda the craftsman in *polimetría*   73

Bibliographical note   79

For Gwilym

Preface

A fragment of *El estudiante de Salamanca* appeared in print for the first time in 1836, when readers of the issue of *El Español* for 7 March (no. 128) were presented with a section of Part I. In 1837 and 1839 two more pre-publication releases (*Museo Artístico y Literario*, no. 4, 22 June 1837, 26-8; *La Alhambra* (published by the Asociación Literaria de Granada), II, no. 3, 30 June 1839, 33) further whetted the appetite of the public, and the complete poem was included in the *Poesías* of 1840.

References to the text of *El estudiante de Salamanca* are to the 1971 reprint of the Clásicos Castellanos volume, *Espronceda. Poesías. El estudiante de Salamanca* (Madrid, 1923), edited by José Moreno Villa. The form of reference used – e.g. (232:18) – shows the page number followed by the number of the line on the page. Lines are numbered separately for each page in the edition cited, where the numbering includes lines occupied by headings and epigraphs (these account for breaks in the numerical sequence of references in my review of the whole text in the appendix on versification).

The figures in italic type refer to the numbered items in the Bibliographical Note.

In conformity with editorial practice in this series as regards quotation in languages other than English and Spanish, I have provided translations in the footnotes.

I should like to thank Professor Varey and Professor Deyermond for the help they have given me ever since the time when they allowed a stray from another department into their lectures.

1 Introduction

The complaint is occasionally heard that some commentators on nineteenth-century literature spend too long trying to interpret every detail of the written word in terms of an author's experiences and personality. A study of this length is clearly not the place to trace Espronceda's doings from his first breath to his last, but if *El estudiante de Salamanca* is isolated from its creator it may leave unanswered questions in some readers' minds. The main character of the poem is a jaunty superman, bristling with rebellion and unwavering bravado, leaving a trail of broken hearts in his wake with a callousness worthy of his forerunner in Tirso's *El burlador de Sevilla*. Yet momentarily there appears in the wings a shadowy commentator whose voice is full of despair and who speaks of such a deep love for one individual woman that the foundering of this relationship has plunged him into total world-weariness. Was the legend that grew up around Espronceda right to identify him with Don Félix de Montemar, or is it his voice we hear in the few stanzas interposed by the commentator in Part IV? Is it closer to the truth to find a facet of him in both these apparently antithetical figures, just as Alfred de Musset mirrored the two halves of himself in the melancholy lover and the roistering debauchee who are the joint heroes of *Les Caprices de Marianne*?

Even nowadays it is not easy to feel that we can come as close to Espronceda as biographers such as André Maurois and V.S. Pritchett bring us to Hugo and Balzac. Robert Marrast has carried out a herculean task in excavating new information and in disentangling reality from the myths which helped to make Espronceda's life-story read like the most ultra of ultra-Romantic novels. Yet even he finds himself frustrated, for instance, by the veil of discretion with which Espronceda's contemporaries and early biographers hid many of the precise details about the history of his relationship with Teresa Mancha, so that facts which might once have embarrassed the poet's descendants may now be lost for ever. Apart from the sparseness of even basic biographical knowledge about his comings and goings, there seems to be a comparative dearth of the material such as memoirs and correspondence which, in the biographies of English or

French nineteenth-century men of note, clothe the bones of facts with the flesh of feelings and thoughts.

Tantalising though this is, we know enough of his life to understand how easily even contemporary eyes could see him as the sort of flamboyant, rebellious human stuff from which Don Juans are formed. Certainly there is enough adventure in his thirty-four years of existence to furnish a Rafael Sabatini or an Ian Fleming with more than one action-packed plot. At the same time, psychologists might perhaps read into the same course of events factors that explain the despair of later years. Like the "génération ardente, pâle, nerveuse" that Musset analyses in his *Confession d'un enfant du siècle* (Part I, chapter 2), Espronceda was a child of war. "Tous ces enfants étaient des gouttes d'un sang brûlant qui avait inondé la terre; ils étaient nés au sein de la guerre, pour la guerre."[1] For Musset, the Napoleonic wars and their aftermath were a major cause of hopelessness and cynicism in the young Frenchmen of his era, and it could be argued that Espronceda was more directly involved than them in a war which moved on to Spanish soil in the very year of his birth. If there is any truth in twentieth-century French obstetricians' theories about the lasting influence on a child of the circumstances in which it is born, Espronceda seems predisposed from his first moments to a life of turbulence and insecurity. The well-known story tells how his birth occurred as an emergency as his father's cavalry regiment rode towards Badajoz, the motion of his mother's carriage evidently being as efficient as the bouncing and bucking of modern ambulances in inducing and shortening labour. Although it is a pity to discard the legend that he was delivered in a shepherd's hut, the palace of a hospitable nobleman is almost as suitable a birthplace for a Romantic poet and, after a birth as sudden as the skeletons' dance in *El estudiante de Salamanca*, an early biographer soon had José riding at his father's side to face the French troops, an army cadet already at the age of five or six (*23*, p. 9). Unfortunately no documentary evidence has so far proved that his childhood was spent in this dramatic way, and one of the

---

[1] Musset, *Œuvres complètes*, ed. Philippe van Tieghem, L'Intégrale (Paris, 1963), p. 555. "All these children were drops of a fiery blood which had drenched the earth; they were born in the midst of war, for war."

earliest first-hand descriptions of him seems to be Escosura's much-quoted pen-picture of a twelve-year-old tearaway: "aquel niño franco, simpático, gentil, de entendimiento claro, de temperamento sanguíneo y a la violencia propenso, ágil, de ánimo audaz hasta frisar en lo temerario". [2]

Instead of the stultifying calm of at least some of the post-Napoleonic war years in France, a calm in which Musset's "enfants du siècle" sank into despairing apathy, Espronceda lived out a life of adventure in reality rather than in dreams and fiction. Except at the barricades of 1830 (where the Spanish poet joined them), few Frenchmen of the Romantic generation had occasion to draw a weapon in anger, unless in a duel. Espronceda, on the other hand, combined from his late teens till his death the role of man of letters with that of man of action. An embryo Don Félix in his rebelliousness, when just fifteen he met his friends of "Los Numantinos" to plot the downfall of the political regime. Like conspirators in the most exaggerated of Romantic melodramas, they decked one of their meeting-places, a cellar in the calle de Hortaleza, with trappings which strike a note as macabre as Part IV of *El estudiante de Salamanca*. Escosura, the president, tells of the walls and furniture being draped in black, contrasting with the red paper lanterns decorated with the shapes of bones and skulls. On the presidential table were arranged crossed swords and a pair of pistols, and around it gathered his fellow members, masked, their youthful forms enveloped in dark cloaks, daggers in their hands. Any visiting Frenchman of progressive literary tastes would have thought this incarnation of his dreams of Spain too good to be true. Certainly the Espronceda who later wrote the *Canción del pirata* and who invented Don Félix, advancing sword in hand in pursuit of danger, was not a poet whose feet had scarcely stirred from under the safety of a writing-table.

If only more details were available, the years of exile alone would fill a volume with escapades, as he moved from Portugal to England and France, commuting between the last two countries with a Scarlet

---

[2] Patricio de la Escosura, 'Cómo y de qué manera conocí a Espronceda', *La Ilustración Española y Americana*, I, 5 (8 February 1876), 87-90. As quoted in *23*, p.60.

Pimpernel-like elusiveness which at times infuriated the French authorities. It is significant that, while other refugees eked out their finances by giving Spanish lessons, Don Félix's creator earned money by the skill of his sword, as a fencing-master. The French police may have been wrong to see him as a spy when he first reached Paris, but before long he was caught up in a series of political intrigues and adventures. Robert Marrast has put firm foundations under one story, showing that Espronceda did indeed fight at the barricades during "les Trois Glorieuses". Other anecdotes are less well documented, but nevertheless make good telling. One night, for instance, Espronceda is supposed to have fallen exhausted into bed at an inn after shaking off pursuers. It was only on waking that he found he had been sharing his bed with a corpse (*5*, p.xix).

Even after an amnesty allowed him to return to Spain, he still mirrored Don Félix the rebel and also the reveller. The inn scene in Part III of *El estudiante de Salamanca* is a model of decorum compared with the wild deeds of the group known as "la Partida del Trueno". The antics of some of the young writers of the day as they poured out of the Café del Príncipe into the streets of Madrid make the sunset walks of their French counterparts through Paris look like a Sunday School outing. It is intriguing to think that the tragic Larra of *El Día de Difuntos de 1836* once daubed the Duke of Alba's parked carriage bright red to mystify the owner when he came to reclaim it. Espronceda too occasionally amused himself with carriages, tethering them to street-stalls so that the whole contraption clattered away when the driver moved off. Some of the group's misdeeds have a reassuringly modern ring. They broke shop windows and street-lights, fired peashooters at passers-by and arrived uninvited to cause mayhem at gatherings in private houses.[3] Robert Marrast has discovered the report of a December evening in 1835 when Espronceda with a band of friends burst in, unmasked, on a masked ball, caused havoc among the dancers and then leaped on to a table, "en donde escandalosamente brindaron por la República universal, y por la destrucción de todos los tronos; únicos brindis de estos malvados" (*16*, p. 484).

[3] F. Fernández de Córdova, *Mis memorias íntimas*, I, Biblioteca de Autores Españoles, CXCII (Madrid, 1966), pp.91-2, and Larra, 'Los Calaveras', *Revista Mensajero*, 2 and 5 June 1835.

This is Espronceda as contemporary Madrid saw him, the image reinforced by his own words in *A Jarifa en una orgía*, where he calls for caresses and for wine,

> Y aturdan mi revuelta fantasía
> Los brindis y el estruendo del festín,
> Y huya la noche y me sorprenda el día
> En un letargo estúpido y sin fin.

Taken by themselves, this rowdiness (though Espronceda was also involved in far more serious political activities than this demonstration at the ball) and these hints of debauchery seem to justify the view that Don Félix is a self-portrait. What the public perhaps tended to forget was that *A Jarifa en una orgía* is less of a drinking-song than a song of utter despair, and in most of its stanzas it is not *El estudiante de Salamanca*'s Don Félix but its world-weary commentator whose voice is heard. It is true that this second voice is heard for relatively few stanzas in the long dramatic poem, but its tone seems to me to provide the key to the work's basic outlook on life. Don Félix's bravado and humour never fail him for more than a moment, but in the last resort they are of no avail. Superman though he may be, his strength cannot resist the onslaught of a malevolent universe, and his defiance has only the value of an existentialist gesture.

The Espronceda who wrote these twelve revealing stanzas (226:19-228:10) was not the young firebrand known to the public but the man who can be glimpsed in the love-affair which dominated his sentimental life during the years of exile and continued after his return to Spain. At first sight the story of how he fell in love with Teresa Mancha, and eloped with this young wife of a Spanish businessman and mother of two children, to live for a blissfully happy period on the outskirts of Paris, merely confirms impressions that his biography must really be the product of some hyper-romantic imagination, the libretto for a Puccini opera perhaps. Later, after she had been installed in the neighbouring house to his mother's in Madrid, the relationship seems to have sunk into the sort of dreary bickering familiar to Marriage Guidance counsellors. The fact that she ran away from him, was brought back, and left again to live with another man before her early death from consumption (again we have an ultra-romantic vignette in the account of a grief-stricken

Espronceda gazing through the "reja" at her body laid out in a street-level room) is usually explained by her boredom and feeling of neglect when her lover was too preoccupied with politics and literature to spend much time with her. Anyone who has read Part II of *El estudiante de Salamanca*, as well as *A Jarifa en una orgía* and *Canto a Teresa*, would welcome far more information about the end of the love-affair. It seems reasonable to imagine that this may be the source of Espronceda's ambivalent attitude to women — his idealisation of their purity and innocence turning to loathing once they have descended from their pedestal and yielded to a lover.

> Mujeres vi de virginal limpieza
> entre albas nubes de celeste lumbre;
> yo las toqué, y en humo su pureza
> trocarse vi y en lodo y podredumbre.
>
> (*A Jarifa en una orgía*)

Yet this could be as much of an over-simplification as the view that Musset's life fell into ruins solely because of his disastrous relationship with George Sand. Clearly Espronceda did not take refuge in unmitigated cynicism, since when he died he was apparently happily engaged to Bernarda Beruete. Ironically enough, her behaviour after his death met the very highest standards he could have asked of a woman: she never married, and is said to have kept his grave constantly supplied with flowers. As his friends remained discreetly tight-lipped, in print at least, we are left to speculate whether it was shock and bitter disillusionment with the mistress who deserted him which caused the despairing attitude of *El estudiante de Salamanca*'s commentator, and certain aspects of Elvira's portrait, or whether there were other, deeper reasons.

If it is difficult to read the poem without occasionally thinking of the poet, it is almost impossible to see it in isolation from the Romantic movement, typified in Spain by Espronceda and his work. Whole volumes have been devoted to defining Romanticism, and C.S. Lewis for one believed that the word had become so worn through over-handling that it was no longer fit to be part of the currency of present-day criticism. Nevertheless, he offers a list of seven essential facets of Romanticism, a list which provides a valuable yardstick for measuring this quality in *El estudiante de Salamanca*. So aptly does this definition from the preface to the third edition of *The Pilgrim's Regress*[4] apply to the work we are studying that it seems worth while to quote the passage almost in its entirety:

1. Stories about dangerous adventure — particularly, dangerous adventure in the past or in remote places — are "romantic". In this sense Dumas is a typically "romantic" author, and stories about sailing ships, the Foreign Legion, and the rebellion of 1745, are usually "romantic".

2. The marvellous is "romantic", provided it does not make part of the believed religion. Thus magicians, ghosts, fairies, witches, dragons, nymphs, and dwarfs are "romantic"; angels, less so....

3. The art dealing with "Titanic" characters, emotions strained beyond the common pitch, and high-flown sentiments or codes of honour is "romantic"....

4. "Romanticism" can also mean the indulgence in abnormal, and finally in anti-natural, moods. The *macabre* is "romantic", and so is an interest in torture, and a love of death.... In this sense *Tristan* is Wagner's most "romantic" opera; Poe, Baudelaire, and Flaubert, are "romantic" authors; Surrealism is "romantic".

5. Egoism and Subjectivism are "romantic". In this sense the typically "romantic" books are *Werther* and Rousseau's *Confessions*, and the works of Byron and Proust.

6. Every revolt against existing civilisation and conventions whether it look forward to revolution, or backward to the "primitive" is called "romantic" by some people. Thus pseudo-Ossian, Epstein, D.H. Lawrence, Walt Whitman, and Wagner are "romantic".

7. Sensibility to natural objects, when solemn and enthusiastic, is "romantic". In this sense *The Prelude* is the most "romantic" poem in the world: and there is much "romanticism" in Keats, Shelley, de Vigny, de Musset and Goethe.

Statements such as this always inflame argument, both about what they include and what they omit, but it is useful to bear C.S. Lewis's words in mind as we turn to examine Espronceda's poem.

---

[4] Collins Fount Paperbacks, 1977, pp.9-11.

2 *Espronceda the descriptive artist*

There is scarcely any need for a reminder of the importance to a Romantic of the setting in which a work is placed. The archpriest of the French school, Victor Hugo, maintains in his manifesto, the *Préface de Cromwell*, that "les personnages parlants ou agissants ne sont pas les seuls qui gravent dans l'esprit du spectateur la fidèle empreinte des faits"[5] and that a writer must, as an essential part of the creative process, choose characteristic details to paint in each background. This concern for local colour ties in with the movement's love of nature, of the exotic and the vivid, and its interest in the individuality of places and times as well as of people. It is true that this passion for colouring in the setting can be ridiculous if discretion is not used, as Musset underlines in *Namouna* when he satirises literary "Oriental" extravaganzas spangled with gold and silver, with a blue-roofed town, a white mosque, minarets, a red horizon, and a multi-coloured sky. Yet Musset himself had fallen into a similar trap when, as a fledgling dramatist, he sketched a play about Scotland with all the potentially ludicrous contemporary clichés about the land of Ossian and Walter Scott. In fact this Scottish fantasy, *La Quittance du diable*, with its capering skeletons, leads us into almost exactly the same world as the opening of *El estudiante de Salamanca*, except that it takes place in the countryside instead of in a city.

When the curtain rises, in the reader's imagination, on Espronceda's Salamanca it can be seen at once that this is one of the scenarios of international Romanticism. We find ourselves in the long-distant past at midnight, the hour when the dead rise from their tombs, when fearful whispers and hollow footsteps are half-heard. Next we encounter an ingredient imported into a largely ghost-free Spain, for phantoms wander through the darkness to the accompaniment of the howling of terrified dogs and the mysterious clangour of the bell in a ruined church (only buildings in a ruinous state really met with the Romantics' approval), its accursed peals calling witches to their sabbath. The sky is starless, and a wind which might have come straight from the Yorkshire moors of *Wuthering Heights* moans

[5] *La Préface de Cromwell*, ed. Maurice Souriau, Nouvelle Bibliothèque Littéraire (Paris, n.d.), p. 234. "It is not only the characters who speak and move that imprint on the audience's mind a true record of events."

balefully. Against the darkness of the sky even darker silhouettes rear up like black spectres, the shapes of church towers and of the ramparts of the gothic castle whose very sentries are smitten with fear. Clearly the scene that is depicted is not necessarily Salamanca, and it could be argued that, rather than Spain, we see before us the Romantic stereotype of Northern Europe complete with spectres, witches and howling winds. When Tirso's original "burlador de Sevilla" met a ghost in Golden Age Spanish literature, it was a solid apparition of good Spanish stone and not a wraith half-glimpsed in the shadows.

The scenario created at the beginning of this nightmare orchestrated in verse is, then, the stock issue of one certain type of Romantic backdrop. In its own right it strikingly ushers in the themes of violent death and of man faced with the supernatural in a horrific form. When Tirso's Don Juan meets his end at the hands of the statue, readers to a great extent build and furnish the funeral chapel in their own imagination, as did early audiences, with the help of a few accessories provided by the dialogue. On the other hand, when Espronceda's Don Juan-figure and the wraith who is to lead him to his death first appear before us, our imagination is not made redundant, but it is amply fed with shapes and sounds, with varying shades of darkness shot with flashes and flickers of light and colour. This descriptive passage is not an extraneous piece of Romantic bric-à-brac; it fulfils the same function as a successful overture to an opera or a ballet. In this Salamanca which is no more a geographical reality than the Madrid Musset creates in *Contes d'Espagne et d'Italie*, the dying cry which begins the action rings out and the black shape of an *embozado* is glimpsed, slipping into the calle del Ataúd. The name itself could be placarded over many a Romantic dream of Spain and the street lives up to its label, gloomy even in the daytime, lit at night only by the feebly flickering lamp which illuminates a statue of Christ. Even this one source of light is "triste", "ya pronta a espirar", just bright enough to make the drawn sword glitter and to let us see the blood still dripping from its blade. This is the very epitome of the contemporary fashion in plays, poems and novels for introducing a religious note into the setting to intensify tales of the supernatural, of horror and of sudden death. In England Matthew "Monk" Lewis was one of the earliest writers of the horror novel to chill spines with his combination of Spain, religion and violence, and so hackneyed did the theme become that in 1825 a French satirist wrote to an imaginary correspondent:

> J'espère que votre premier soin à Madrid sera de visiter les horribles prisons [of the Inquisition], et de pénétrer toutes les horreurs souterraines et monastiques dont depuis si longtemps nous vivons, nous autres auteurs de romans! J'espère tirer de votre récit d'excellents matériaux ... De grâce, n'oubliez pas non plus ces moines blancs, maigres et lents, que l'on voit fuir, à minuit, un poignard à la main, dans les détours des souterrains humides...[6]

Part II opens with another nocturne, but its atmosphere is very different from the sinister tones of the earlier evocation of Salamanca at night. The first scene, introducing the murderous Don Félix, belonged to the world of witches and ghosts; this second night-piece is as pure and virginal as its heroine before passion destroyed her. (There were, after all, few things the Romantics liked better than a good antithesis.) The horrific townscape has changed to an idyllic garden in the countryside, a moonlit garden with all the melancholy lyricism that Chopin knew how to evoke, or Berlioz in some of his *Nuits d'été*. The moon is as hard-worked in Romantic scenery as thunderstorms, but this is no cardboard moon hung in the sky simply to suit contemporary taste. In fact this is one of the passages which seem to me to challenge some critics' view that Espronceda has no feeling for nature. It is true that moonlit gardens were two-a-penny in the literature of the day (though none the less attractive for that), and that anyone wanting to re-create one in Spanish need look no further than the literary models of Musset's *Nuits* and the closing scene of Hugo's *Hernani,* among countless descriptions by English, French and German writers. To say, nevertheless, that this backdrop for Elvira's first appearance strikes

[6] Théodore Anne (also attributed to V.-J. Etienne de Jouy), *Madrid, ou observations sur les mœurs et les usages des Espagnols au commencement du XIXe siècle,* 2 vols (Paris, 1825), I, pp.278-81. "I hope that your first concern in Madrid will be to visit the horrid prisons [of the Inquisition] and to penetrate all the subterranean, monastic horrors from which we novelists have made our living for so long! I hope to extract excellent material from your account... I beg you too not to forget those white-clad, emaciated, slow-moving monks whom one sees stealing at midnight, dagger in hand, along the winding ways of damp underground passages."

me as having the freshness and detail of personal observation is to risk the immediate discovery that it is no more than the literal translation of some other author's lines, but even if this were so it might still be argued that Espronceda has made them his own as effectively as many a Classical writer or musician has done with a borrowed theme.

The sensual richness of the passage matches that of an orchestral tone-poem or a painting. The composition of the picture leads our eye first to the sky, then to the moonlight moving over a hill-side, to the stream in the middle ground, and finally to the trees and flowers in the foreground. One of the most satisfying aspects is the interplay of varying textures and light effects. In the smooth, filmy gauze of the sky, the moon's "blanca luz süave" turns the stream's waters into a "fúlgida cinta de plata" bordered by the jewel-like glitter of its "franjas de esmeralda". Add to this the reference to stars, and the "argentadas chispas" of glittering water glimpsed through the dark mass of branches, and the whole picture becomes a study in the contrasts of sparkling light with the serene radiance of the moon and sky. It would take an extremely skilled painter's brush to do as much. Colours are not lacking, and again they are taken from a totally different range from those of the duel-scene with its moonless sky, its total gloom relieved only by the flicker of a lamp and by a streak of blood red. Here the colours of violent death are replaced by the virginal white of the moon, orange blossom and acacia, offset by touches of blue, emerald green and silver. To make the parallel closer between landscape and the figure framed in it, the moon is personified as "pura virgen solitaria". Espronceda has done everything that a painter could, but he also adds movement, sound and scent. The stream slips by; the murmuring breezes (not the whistling wind of the earlier scene) stir the flowering bushes and "en perfumes se embalsaman". The poem achieves in words what Falla was to evoke in his *Noches en los jardines de España*.

To Elvira, when the moon's rays light on her, an Ophelia strewing petals in her madness, the night and the garden bring nothing but torture. The murmuring wind and water only accentuate the absence of her lover's voice and his serenade. Night and moon are untouched by her grief as they were by her happiness. (Momentarily at least, Espronceda sides with Vigny against most of the Romantics in his feeling that nature is indifferent to human grief.) Nor can she tolerate the powerlessness of this peace and beauty to soothe her troubles.

> ¿Qué me valen tu calma y tu terneza,
> Tranquila noche, solitaria luna,
> Si no calmáis del hado la crudeza,
> Ni me dais esperanza de fortuna? (201:1-4)

Milk-and-water heroine though she may look, she has at least a touch of the defiance which is said to make Don Félix a symbol of the Romantic failure to come to terms with the conditions of human life.

Nature image upon nature image is used to describe Elvira, and in the last vignette the flowers and the breeze behave more in the general Romantic tradition by feeling for her death. That most Romantic but also Shakespearean tree, the weeping willow, leans over her "en lánguido desmayo"; and if the moonlight had failed to calm her sufferings, the setting sun's last ray now bathes her tomb with peace (204:21-4). Echoes come into the reader's mind of the opening words of the passage describing Ophelia's watery grave: "There is a willow grows aslant a brook".[7] Musset too wrote lines associating a willow tree with a beautiful girl on the point of death, lines which his friends chose to have engraved on his tomb in the Père-Lachaise cemetery:

> Mes chers amis, quand je mourrai,
> Plantez un saule au cimetière.
> J'aime son feuillage éploré;
> La pâleur m'en est douce et chère,
> Et son ombre sera légère
> A la terre où je dormirai.
>
> (*Lucie*, stanza 1)[8]

Part III introduces another antithesis in setting. This time the scene is an interior, but not very different in colouring and atmosphere from the earlier street episode. Again wan lamplight

---

[7] *Hamlet, Prince of Denmark*, Act IV, scene 7.

[8] "My dear friends, when I die plant a willow in the cemetery. I love its weeping foliage. Its pallor is sweet and dear to me, and its shadow will lie lightly on the earth where I shall be sleeping."

flickers over surrounding darkness, on this occasion the smoke-blackened walls of a tavern, and again evil is invoked—the place is "hellish". Even in these few short stanzas Espronceda takes the trouble to paint in details so that the reader can both see and hear what is going on; we see the expressions on the gamblers' faces, and are aware of the silence broken only by the chink of coins, by oaths and the roaring of the wind that shakes the window panes (205:12-206:8).

This brief sketch which serves as a background to a canto largely made up of dialogue leads us to an astounding piece of virtuoso writing that forms Part IV, astounding both in the quality of its achievement and in the length for which it is sustained. In the face of such sheer brilliance, it is a temptation for the commentator simply to lay down his pen, leaving the passage to speak for itself. Nevertheless, let us look again at Don Félix in the calle del Ataúd.

As he advances down the street, he is setting out to join a nineteenth-century version of the Dance of Death, the dance or procession in which the living are joined by skeletons or by a single figure representing death. In its measures the sinful "have before their eyes the inexorable march of time with Death ghoulishly guiding them to their everlasting doom".[9] From France, where it seems to have originated, the Dance probably reached Iberian literature in the fifteenth century (see *27*, pp.41-50 for its history in Spain). In England John Stow's *A Survey of London* (1598) describes "the Daunce of Machabray, or Dance of Death, commonly called the Dance of [St] Paul's", which included a poem translated from the French by John Lydgate, monk of Bury, and also "the picture of death leading all estates, painted about the cloister, at the dispence of Jenken Carpenter, in the reign of Henry VIth".[10] James M. Clark records two places in Britain where illustrations of the theme are still preserved — at Hexham Priory in Northumberland and in the Parish Church of Newark-on-Trent (*27*, pp.7-8)—and there were other such

---

[9] Leonard P. Kurtz, *The Dance of Death and the Macabre Spirit in European Literature* (New York, 1934; repr. Geneva: Slatkine, 1975), p.281.

[10] Ed. William J. Thoms (London: Whittaker, 1842), p. 122. The painting was destroyed in 1549.

paintings throughout Western Europe. The oldest known example of both pictures and verses could be found on the walls of the Cemetery of the Innocents in Paris until 1669, when the wall which it occupied stood in the way of one of Louis XIV's road-widening projects. The words and illustrations were reproduced in the first edition of the "Dance Macabré", printed in Paris in September 1485. It has been suggested that the plague which swept Europe might have helped to inspire the Dances of Death, as might the witches' sabbaths of mediaeval Europe. Kurtz describes how, in the eleventh century already, the really diabolical "sabbat" was prevalent, "those great nocturnal séances in outlying places in which men, women and children, invoking the demons, devoted themselves to Satan body and soul" (p. 16). This was the famous "ronde" of the "sabbat" – a weird, wild dance whose frenzy is recaptured by *El estudiante de Salamanca*'s skeletons. Nor was the phenomenon confined to plague-ridden Europe with its witches. Kurtz states that nine dancers with skeleton masks take part in ancient religious rituals in Tibet, for instance.

This was exactly the type of subject-matter calculated to appeal to the nineteenth century. The theme had already found its greatest exponent, Holbein, in the Renaissance, but after 1800 the names of its interpreters are legion. Liszt has a *Totentanz* composed in 1849; Saint-Saëns a *Danse macabre* (1874) in which a satanic violinist raises the dead from their graves; Berlioz his *Symphonie fantastique* whose fifth section, "Dream of a Witches' Sabbath", has a Dance of Death based on the "Dies Irae". As for literature, Scott and Browning in England and Poe in America added their versions, while in France a translation helped to make known a much earlier tale by the German G.A. Bürger, whose hero became entrapped in a skeleton dance and himself turned into a skeleton; and in France the public lapped up such stories, both in translation and in original versions by its own authors.[11]

Handled with less than masterly skill, nineteenth-century versions of the theme stay at the entertainment level of a ride on a fairground

[11]See Karl Petit, *Le Livre d'or du Romantisme, anthologie thématique du Romantisme européen*, Collection Marabout Université, CLIII (Verviers, 1968), pp.188-202.

ghost-train, and can strike a twentieth-century reader or listener as ludicrous rather than spine-chilling. Where Espronceda seems to me to succeed is in his recapturing of the phantasmagoric, shifting world of the senses into which his hero is flung, a world where dimensions are as nightmarishly changeful as in surrealist art or literature, as in a Dalí painting or one of Arrabal's "labyrinths" in his *Celebrando la ceremonia de la confusión*. The capering skeletons in Musset's *La Quittance du Diable* may make the reader smile; if a similar type of scene in *El estudiante de Salamanca* catches the same reader up, however unwilling he may be, in its wild round, it is probably partly because he is made to feel each of the sensations that crowd in upon the hero in crescendo. However fantastic the story, the physical feelings of strangeness, hallucination and vertigo could not be more realistically conveyed, even if Espronceda had all the technical resources of Buñuel or Pasolini at his disposal. Don Félix may feel little fear, but not all readers are so immune to the effects that are created.

After the flash-back to Elvira's death and her brother's challenge to her seducer, we are back in the calle del Ataúd. Everything is low-key. Just as Saint-Saëns starts with a mere whisper of sound in the *Danse macabre* which builds up to a frenzied climax, so Espronceda preludes his maelstrom with stillness and darkness; the only movement is that of Don Félix uncertainly making his way through the gloom, and the only light the dying glimmer of the lamp by the statue of Christ. The first sound in what is to become a cataclysmic din is a single sigh, which we not only hear but are made to feel by proxy:

> Resbalar por su faz sintió el aliento,
>
> Y a su pesar sus nervios se crisparon. (222:5-6)

Even film studios have not yet such effects at their disposal. The assault on the hero's senses continues when the phantom woman makes her appearance. This is no comparatively solid and stable ghost like a flesh-and-blood guest disguised at a Hallowe'en party, but "flotante y vaga", a star-like glitter in the distance (222: 17-24), so that Montemar questions for a moment whether it is an illusion or even whether, for once in a lifetime, wine is affecting him. This suggestion is immediately rejected; the "dance of death" in the following lines was not meant to be taken as the Spanish equivalent of the drunkard Scot's ride in Burns's *Tam o' Shanter*. The super-natural, which was merely a suggested presence in Part I, is in full command now. As Don Félix utters his challenge to the devil, the failing lamp flares up, and the spectre zooms in with phantasmagoric effect, changing from a silvery white speck in the distance to a life-size woman kneeling before the sacred image. The battery on his mind continues. As he moves forward, so do the lamp, the statue and the kneeling figure, only to stop when he does. While tears stream from the sculpted Christ's face, the street itself seems to shift and give way beneath him. In small doses, sensory distortions like this are well-established ways of providing fairground thrills in countless "Noah's Arks" and "Crazy Houses", but in more sinister form they are part of the stuff of nightmares (as in Arrabal's *Celebrando la ceremonia de la confusión*), mirages, visual disturbances that occur on the verge of sleep and brain-washing techniques. When a gust of wind blows out the flame as Don Félix's sacrilegious hand reaches out for the lamp, the wraith moves off into the darkness, still bewildering with its billowing draperies and sound-less steps, moving, says Espronceda a few stanzas later, like a "sylphide" who scarcely ripples the lake waters. The ghosts of Part I have been joined in this image by another recruit from Romanticised Northern Europe. After her first spectral sigh, the next sound we hear from her is the groan which prompts the poet to dwell for some sixteen stanzas on the sorrows and disillusionment of love.

When Don Félix rejects her warnings, the prelude is over and the pursuit begins in earnest. He is led on as relentlessly as was the Flying Dutchman through a terrifying night-time cityscape. Streets, squares, walls—"tristes", "solitarias" and "arruinadas"— spin before his eyes, and the sounds that meet his ears are not reassuring. A witch sings in a cracked voice, hollow footsteps of the dead risen from their tomb echo, and the north wind roars over the silent city (230:19-231:8). The pace increases until the reader's head is spinning with Montemar's, as street follows street and square follows square. The verbs of motion pile up, adding to the breathless effect. The two figures "cruzan", "nunca dejan de andar", "atraviesan, pasan, vuelven", "siempre adelante van", and almost every phrase helps to pile on the pressure —"más allá y más allá", "paso tras paso", "una calle y otra", "cien calles", "otras calles, otras plazas recorre y otra ciudad" (231:9-22).

Now the phantasmagoria well and truly comes into its own. In Part I dark towers had loomed like ghosts but at least they were motionless. Those he sees in this unknown and terrifying city contribute to the assault on his mind by leaving their foundations and moving about, circled by a hundred slowly cavorting skeletons who foreshadow the final dance of death. Even the weathercocks add to the sensory confusion by bowing as he passes, and as always Espronceda intensifies the total impression with sound effects. As the black shapes of the towers move, like massive versions of Tirso's avenging statue, the bells clang out mysteriously, all the more terrifying for being personified, their hundred metal tongues repeating Don Félix's name as they echo. All of a sudden, the clangour and confusion are replaced by an equally fearful emptiness, a silent desert, "sin luz, sin aire, sin cielo" (232:18), the thick darkness lit up by melodramatic snakes of lightning in which the ghostly woman's face glows like phosphorus—again demonstrating Espronceda's love of contrast. Whether the reader's tendencies are toward claustrophobia or agoraphobia there is no escape for him in this Romantic equivalent of Dante's *Inferno*.

The phantasmagoria disappears, familiar Salamanca is around him again and Don Félix, groping through the darkness to follow the wraith, finds himself witnessing a spectacle not unknown in the literature of the day—his own funeral. The scene may not be new, but again Espronceda shows himself a master at describing sounds and sights. Not every critic recognises claims that sound can echo and enhance the meaning of a word, but if any lines could prove that this is the case Espronceda must come close to doing so with his:

> Rechinan girando las férreas veletas,
>
> Crujir de cadenas se escuchan sonar. (234:18-19)

Warning after warning rejected, Don Félix is now on the threshold of the final horror of the house where the dance of his death is to take place. One would have thought that the climax of terror already reached could not be surpassed, but Espronceda has scarcely begun. Macabre touches come crowding in. Again the ground shifts; the wings of the night birds beloved of melodrama and ghost stories flap overhead; and blazing eyes glare fixedly out of the darkness.

It is unfortunate that twentieth-century technology with its invention of the photo-electric cell has destroyed the eerie effect of the great doors which seem to open by themselves, but once inside the chills and thrills remain the same as those that the first readers experienced. The mansion of death is evoked as terrifyingly as the mysterious city. We see the shapes – arches, urns, statues, columns, courtyards – all ruinous and speaking of death and decay; we see too the glowing red eyes of the denizens of this "negra, funeral guarida", advancing and retreating as if in some ghastly country-dance, to inspect the intruder. We are made aware of the light by which we see them, the livid, shadow-casting flicker of candles, and of the glacial, heart-chilling silence which surrounds them. All this is a highly effective use of elements in vogue at the period, but again Espronceda adds horror in a form that was to be used by surrealism and by the twentieth century in general. A haunted house that remained static would have inspired less fear than this wavering horror:

> Todo vago, quimérico y sombrío,
> Edificio sin base ni cimiento
> Ondula cual fantástico navío
> Que anclado mueve borrascoso viento. (239:29-240:2)

Not only matter is affected but time too:

> callado,
> Corre allí el tiempo, en sueño sepultado.
>
> Las muertas horas a las muertas horas
> Siguen en el reloj de aquella vida. (240:5-8)

Individual concepts of what is frightening obviously vary, but for some readers one of the strokes of genius in this catalogue of menace must be the description of Don Félix's dizzy descent of the black marble staircase which spirals apparently into infinity, like some crazy circular escalator, so that eventually even this titanic hero's feet slip from under him and he rolls cursing from stair to stair, while beneath him whirl the gyrating shapes of the skeleton dancers and in his ears rings the caterwauling of their jeers. Within four lines Espronceda uses thirteen nouns to represent the sounds they make; and this is not Romantic wordiness but a skilful means of conveying confused cacophony. For me at least it is never possible to read these stanzas without feeling the physical symptoms they aim to produce, and since fear of falling is said to be one of the first instinctive fears, the passage illustrates the way in which the poem sometimes attacks more basic emotions than just man's dread of the supernatural. Again a contrast follows, with the confused mêlée replaced by the single shape of the wraith seated at the foot of the black tomb-cum-marriage-bed.

The feat of descriptive writing that ensues deserves to be one of the best known in Spanish verse. The dance of death proper consists of three stages. First a mere thread of sound and movement grows to a frenzied climax like a full symphony orchestra playing fortissimo; then follows a plateau of narrative; finally the storm of sound and whirling shapes gradually ebbs with Don Félix's strength and dies with him. Skill of this order is perhaps difficult to analyse since every element in the passage seems to fuse with effortless inevitability, but at least three tools are at work in producing the total effect—the manipulation of line lengths so that the physical shape of the poem on the page pictures its contents; the choice of words whose actual sound echoes what they describe; and the use of imagery to convey the desired impression.

The first device was not a new invention. Hugo, for instance, in *Les Djinns*, has on a lesser scale gradually lengthening and then diminishing lines to portray the crescendo and diminuendo of sound and action as a horde approaches the narrator and disappears into the darkness. Yet such experiments with the physical shape of poems are far more common in the twentieth century as, for example, when Pierre Garnier in his "Soleil mystique" (in *Spatialisme et poésie concrète*, 1968) sends lines of words radiating out from the centre of the page to represent the sun's rays, or when Apollinaire composes *La Colombe poignardée et le jet d'eau* with lines which form the outline of a dove and a fountain (*Calligrammes*, 1918). In this sustained experiment with technique Espronceda is more forward-looking than one would expect from some critics' categorisation of him as a representative of Romantic rhetoric.

The first stanzas of the dance of death start, then, with the merest suspicion of sound. Just as the ideal introductory organ voluntary is said to be the nearest thing possible to silence, so Espronceda catches the first gradation of audible sound with six lines, each containing only one stressed syllable:

Fúnebre

Llanto

> De amor,
> Oyese
> En tanto
> En son ... (245:13-18)

This is matched by the last stanza of all, before the final coda brings the reader back to the world of daylight and normality:

> Leve,
> Breve
> Son. (255:9-11)

To add to the symmetry, the same image is used in both the opening and closing pairs of stanzas, just as Saint-Saëns uses the same haunting phrase of music at the start and end of his *Chanson triste*, depicting rising and ebbing frenzy in the dance of a dying woman. The second stanza, a shade longer in length and number of lines, compares the sound Don Félix hears, a love-stricken lament, to a fading sigh. In the next to the last stanza, as he himself dies, he hears the echo of another such sigh, like the sighing of a lyre stirred by a breath. Whether these stanzas are read aloud or silently, the brevity of the lines and the actual sound of the words chosen— "llanto", "flébil", "blando"—impose the pace and volume that Espronceda wished.

The lines grow steadily longer, keeping pace as the volume builds up inexorably. In the third stanza the music, described with softly-sounding words such as "murmullo" and "arrullo", invites as a simile the memory of long-distant love, since both produce the same melancholy. Here the sound is "lánguida y vaga", "dulce", but gradually throughout the following stanza the force increases. The "cántico ideal" of stanza three, in stanza four "en sonoras ráfagas / Aumentado va" (246:15-16). A "rumor prodigioso", it is still no more than the ghostly echo of distant music but it presages the din of a storm, and in the later part of the stanza the noise is evoked by "bramando", "rugido", "estrépito". The imagery helps to intensify the building climax. The sigh of the first stanzas is now the gust beginning to stir the tree-tops as a hurricane approaches; the ocean waves are whipped up and a wall groans in the oncoming storm.

The next three stanzas continue the pattern of direct statement about the swelling sound —"los lúgubres sonidos / Más cerca vanse oyendo" (247:7-8); "y el ruido / Más cerca crece" (247:22-3);

"el estrépito crece / Confuso y mezclado en un son" (248:4-5). The statements are combined with illustrative images. The sound becomes a hollow roar like thunder echoing round mountains or like the rumbling of a volcano. Then, in the orchestral sound, the rest of the percussion joins the drums. In Saint-Saëns's *Carnaval des animaux* the xylophone represents the clatter of the skeleton dance, but it could not surpass the imitative effect of Espronceda's "algazara y gritería, / Crujir de afilados huesos / Rechinamiento de dientes" (247:14-16), or his "Escucha chocarse cráneos, / Ya descarnados y secos" (247:24-5). Winds, waves and thunder reach the same paroxysm, until in the next stanza the confusion is focused into one still louder note:

> Que ronco en las bóvedas hondas
> Tronando furioso zumbó;
> Y un eco que agudo parece
> Del ángel del juicio la voz
> En tiple, punzante alarido
> Medroso y sonoro se alzó. (248:6-11)

There is no need to argue the case that a succession of long vowels, especially "o", produces a sonorous sound when Espronceda provides the proof by so conclusively pulling out the trumpet stop, nor to plead the percussive effect of plosive consonants after reading his "crujir a sus pies con fragor, / Chocar en las piedras los cráneos" (248:13-14). *El diablo mundo* repeats this virtuoso recapturing in verse of the noise, movement and spectacle of a supernatural horde in motion, though on a smaller scale than here.[12]

The dead have risen at the trumpet blast and it is in a frenzy of sound unthinkable before the twentieth century produced discothèques that Don Félix finds himself the focus of a hundred skeletons' hollow eyes and pointing fingers. After this cleverly controlled progression of sound effects in words, Espronceda devotes himself to sending chills down his reader's spine by evoking the physical sensations of touch. The lines have settled to a uniform length for the narrative section in which the three main characters face each other against the background of the encircling skeletons. The dénouement of *El burlador de Sevilla* reaches its terrifying

---

[12]The passage in *El diablo mundo* comprises nine stanzas, from "Como zumba sonante a lo lejos" to "Y oír y ver piensa después que pasó" (5, pp.89-90).

climax as Don Juan is gripped by the stone Commander's hand; here Don Félix, taking the hand of the veiled figure, finds that "era su tacto de crispante hielo".

> Galvánica, cruel, nerviosa y fría,
> Histérica y horrible sensación,
> Toda la sangre coagulada envía
> Agolpada y helada al corazón... (249:9-12)

In this short passage a series of words —"crispante", "hielo", "fría", "coagulada", "helada"— suggest the iciness of touch, and the hard-sounding consonants throughout the lines seem to recapture the shock of its impact on Don Félix's nervous system. Soon it is not just the touch of a skeletal hand that is being described, but the loathsome embrace that pinions him. One would have thought that all the word-effects to conjure up dry bones had already been exhausted, but in this stanza a succession of hard "c" sounds helps to convey the feel of the bony limbs, and the repeated vowels "o" and "a" in "ávido", "boca", "cavernosa", "busca", "árida" and "descarnada" seem to gape like the fleshless mouth which bears down on Don Félix.

> El cariädo, lívido esqueleto,
> Los fríos, largos y asquerosos brazos,
> Le enreda en tanto en apretados lazos,
> Y ávido le acaricia en su ansiedad.
> Y con su boca cavernosa busca
> La boca a Montemar, y a su mejilla
> La árida, descarnada y amarilla
> Junta y refriega repugnante faz. (251:5-12)

"Amarilla" adds a nauseating touch to Doña Elvira's picture, and a few lines earlier Don Diego contributes a melodramatic splash of colour with his golden spurs, corpse-pale face, and the blood still flowing from his chest wounds.

Once Don Félix is in his ghostly bride's clutches, the skeleton horde comes into the foreground again and the verses concentrate on the ever-whirling dance which accompanies their macabre wedding song. As the earlier stanzas described sound, now it is movement which is depicted with supreme skill. Again images contribute. The spectres spin round like eddying dust, or dead leaves driven by the wind. Mostly, however, the effect is conjured up by the piling of word upon word denoting phantasmagoric speed, until the pressure of horrific sights and sounds combined with his bride's crushing embrace finally triumphs over Don Félix's physical strength. Darkness and light, the room and its spectres spin before his eyes, and four stanzas taper gradually away almost to nothingness with his ebbing strength, with the flickering of a shortlived flame, and with the fading echo of a dying sigh which had been the first sound heard in his dance of death. After their fearsome crescendo and climax sound and movement are both stilled, with the hero's life, in what must be one of the shortest stanzas in Spanish poetry (255:9-11).

With a mere change of metre Espronceda signals a change of scene as effectively as if he had dropped a theatre curtain and raised it on a different backdrop. The coda section is a complete contrast to the terrible nocturne which has just ended. The dawn touches the clouds with warm colour, "de carmín y grana" (255:12), and emblazons towers which in the preceding nightmare had been macabre, perambulating bulks. The adjectives here are "alegre", "sereno", "calma", "blanda" and "celestial", and the night-time wraiths have given way to the everyday bustle of the city.

In its many contrasts, *El estudiante de Salamanca* shows Espronceda to be a past master in the art of playing with words upon all our senses. The type of ghostly tale he tells can seem hilariously funny to a later generation which nevertheless is prepared to sit transfixed while being pleasantly terrified by exactly the same sort of themes – the menace of the unknown, alarming changes of space, time or perspective – transferred to the fashionable realm of science fiction and to cinema and television. This can only be a personal judgment, but it seems to me that, whereas Lewis's *The Monk* can be read in bed as a comic, post-flu tonic, and even early Frankenstein films provoke grins instead of shivers, *El estudiante de Salamanca* still produces its intended reaction. Perhaps this is due partly to sheer technical genius and partly to the fact that Espronceda knows how to tap some of man's elemental fears. Given a literary vengeance-wreaking ghost who is comparatively substantial and static, twentieth-century readers tend to be sceptical; but presented with a kaleidoscopic, menacing world of shifting shapes, changing perspectives and familiar scenes become unfamiliar, many will recognise fragments of their own nightmares.

Whatever conflicts of opinion there may be about Don Félix de Montemar, few people are likely to challenge the view that he is one of the outstanding figures among the multitudes of beings created by Spanish fiction. It could certainly be argued that he would be one of the most favoured contestants in a competition to find the greatest Spanish Romantic hero, although perhaps no invented character fills that bill as well as do the flesh-and-blood Espronceda and Larra. Different aspects of Don Félix's role have been variously stressed by critics. There is the Don Félix whom Espronceda himself maintains is of the lineage of Don Juan, the "burlador de Sevilla". At least as important is Don Félix the personification of Romantic rebellion, the "trascendentalización del yo" as Casalduero calls him (*9*, p. 172), who carries the revolt of the poet's earlier heroes — the pirate, the beggar and the cossack — into the realm of religion and who is the only Don Juan figure in Spanish literature to defy God and the devil to the very end. Even Tirso's Don Juan calls for a confessor in his last moments, though to no avail. Spanish Romanticism rarely overshadows the movement in the rest of Western Europe, but at this summit of defiance Don Félix rivals Byron's, Hugo's and Schiller's outcasts from society. Only Lucifer, revived as a literary hero in this period, surpasses him, but it is difficult to think of a major nineteenth-century work in which he occupies the leading role, and in any case Don Félix differs from him in representing a man's, rather than a spirit's, challenge to God.

Another facet of Don Félix which soon struck his readers was the family resemblance he bore to his author, to the riotous reveller whose exploits gave rise to the "leyenda roja" surrounding him, just as Byron's and Musset's public had followed agog these author-aristocrats' trail of debauchery and attempts to scandalise the bourgeoisie on every possible occasion. Ferrer del Río, describing Espronceda, comments that with "su inmenso raudal de vida se desbordó con furia gastando su ardor bizarro en desenfrenados placeres y crapulosos festines: a haber poseído inmensos caudales fuera el Don Juan Tenorio del siglo diecinueve ... El estudiante de Salamanca dibuja en Don Félix de Montemar su propio retrato".[13]

[13] *Galería de la literatura española* (Madrid, 1846), pp.242-3.

This mirror-image of an author in his work was, after all, a key characteristic of the Romantic age, when a poet's own life-blood was supposed to be the best nourishment for his writings, when Byron rollicked in various costumes through his own verses, and Musset provided in his theatre a whole portrait-gallery of himself seen from different angles. Yet, even though it is risky to question contemporary testimony that the hero is the creator's double, we shall see that differences emerge between the two. Other students have wondered if Don Félix were not just a Spanish twin of Byron's Don Juan, although a similar relationship with some of Musset's and Leopardi's characters might also be argued.

Amid this cloud of theorising, it would probably be best to concentrate on the actual figure of Don Félix as he makes his way through the poem. At his first entry, a mysterious "embozado" with his hat pulled down over his eyes (a costume the French Romantics themselves loved to adopt for evening sorties in Paris), his drawn sword dripping blood, he advances serenely towards an apparition that would have struck terror into the most fearless and most irreligious of men.

From Don Félix's first appearance to his last gasp of breath, it is this fearlessness, both physical and metaphysical, which is hammered home. In the swaggering stanzas in Part I where Espronceda halts the action to give a portrait of his hero, we are told that his courage is unshakeable, buttressed as it is by complete confidence in his valour and his swordsmanship. This, then, is the invincible man of action who has been the stuff of which heroes are made from the earliest days of story-telling until the present, when John Wayne or the men of World War Two rivet millions of eyes to the television screen. Many Romantic heroes share this courage but very few could claim, as Don Félix does, that he contemplates the future with as much calmness as the present and never spares a remorseful thought for the past with its forsaken women and gambling losses. It is very hard to think of a character in European Romantic literature who is not in some way a tortured introspective, sometimes lamenting with Hernani and Don Alvaro the fate that has misshapen his life and fearing his accursed effect in the future on those he loves.[14] Perhaps

[14] See Victor Hugo, *Hernani*, Act I, scene 2, and the Duque de Rivas, *Don Alvaro, o la fuerza del sino*, Act III, scene 3.

the most powerful study of self-torture is Musset's Lorenzaccio, in the play of that name, a man reduced to a physical wreck and to agony of mind over the debauched ways which he has had to adopt to penetrate the defences of the tyrant he intends to kill. Don Félix too makes his daily life a round of seduction and orgies, but with an untroubled conscience and with positive enjoyment.

This, then, is that most unusual specimen—a cheerful Romantic hero, mingling "un chiste a una maldición" (193:12), as bent on pleasure as Tirso's "Burlador". To add to his attractions, his cheerfulness expresses itself in wit, so that we have the irresistible combination of courage and sardonic humour. Byron's and Musset's leading men are witty too, but their humour is usually tinged with at least passing moods of melancholy. Mario Praz mentions the "pale face furrowed by an ancient grief" characteristic of Byronic heroes (*29*, p.66). It is true that Zorrilla's Don Juan also revels his way through the first scenes of the play, but after falling in love with Inés he is reduced to the usual gloom and despondency of the weeping-willow type of lover.

Again Don Félix stands apart from a good many of his contemporaries in fiction in that he most decidedly does not play the role of a lover worshipping at the foot of his beloved's pedestal:

> Corazón gastado, mofa
> De la mujer que corteja,
> Y, hoy despreciándola, deja
> La que ayer se le rindió. (192:25-8)

This was a time when love between man and woman was idealised almost to the point of becoming a religion, and it was in fact exalted in Zorrilla's version of the Don Juan theme to the level of a redemptive power which snatches the hero back from the mouth of Hell as he places his hand in that of the ghostly novice who was willing to bargain her soul for his salvation (see the final act of *Don Juan Tenorio*). Unlike the "homme fatal" who grieves for the beauties destroyed by him, unlike Casanova who is said to have been genuinely fond of many of the women he encountered, Don Félix goes on his way with unwavering callousness. The way in which Elvira is portrayed may provide a clue as to how far he is a replica of his creator, but it is worth remembering that the Espronceda of the pornographic poems recorded by Cascales Muñoz in *El auténtico*

Espronceda pornográfico y el apócrifo en general (1932) seems highly likely to have been capable of adopting Don Félix's cavalier attitude to women. Clearly this is not an Espronceda who has found his Teresa, unless he represents the Espronceda who has seen his idealising love turn to scorn. Idealisation and contempt are after all a perhaps not uncommon paradox in Iberian men's attitude to females.

Heartless as the "Burlador" in his treatment of women, Don Félix is far more positive than his prototype in his flouting of religion. Tirso's Don Juan gives the impression that he simply averts his mind from God and hell fire for the time being because such thoughts are inconvenient. He is ready enough to dismiss earthly authority contemptuously but when the moment of divine reckoning comes his call for a confessor shows that he is a backsliding believer and not an unbeliever. Don Félix is certainly not a Romantic atheist; rather he is an impious blasphemer whom the unfolding narrative reveals to be obsessed with the need to challenge both God and the devil. The satanic hero was immensely popular at this time; Zorrilla's Don Juan is portrayed as the devil incarnate before his conversion to the love of a good woman. But though Don Félix displays some satanic qualities, he remains resolutely human. He is a titanic being:

> Que hasta en sus crímenes mismos,
> En su impiedad y altiveza,
> Pone un sello de grandeza
> Don Félix de Montemar (193:25-8)

yet superhuman rather than supernatural. He is a Promethean figure, representing human vitality and rebellion flowing at their fastest, and channelled against both Heaven and Hell.

This, then, is Espronceda's introductory portrait of his hero who in addition possesses three attributes essential to any Don Juan – noble blood, wealth, and good looks. In the early nineteenth century, when description tended to run riot, it is perhaps surprising that we are given no details at all of his appearance, but this scarcely matters since for most of the action he is a cloaked silhouette moving through thick darkness. Certainly, if Espronceda meant him to be a symbol of human rebellion, symbols do not need features and readers who create them in their own imagination probably agree with the child who is said to have preferred radio to television "because he liked the pictures better".

How does the rest of the poem bear out this early character study? Part III, giving us a glimpse of Don Félix in the gambling den which was part of his natural habitat, intensifies the picture of an engagingly raffish and heartless cad, of the type whose path has been strewn with broken hearts from the days of mediaeval ballads to those of second-rate magazine stories. Making his entry he cuts an elegant, though still vaguely described, figure:

> Galán de talle gentil,
> La mano izquierda apoyada
> En el pomo de la espada
> Y el aspecto varonil. (207:16-19)

From his first appearance to his last, his sword is symbolically in evidence, a Castilian equivalent of Homeric epithets such as "Hector of the waving plume". Elvira's jewel-framed portrait is soon wagered away and Don Félix makes it clear that the girl herself would follow suit if he had his way:

> No la quiero.
> Mirad si me dais dinero,
> Y os la lleváis (213:2-4)

to which he adds,"¿Queréis la dama? Os la vendo" (213:13). Cavalier treatment of this sort had already half-horrified and half-thrilled contemporary women when they heard stories of how Byron had treated his wife on their wedding night or during childbirth. Yet, quixotically, Don Félix takes umbrage when one of his fellow-gamblers seems to speak slightingly of the beauty in the portrait (213:16-19).

Not suprisingly Don Diego meets with short shrift when he comes to demand vengeance for his sister. Greeted with cold sarcasm —

> Buen hombre, ¿de qué tapiz
> Se ha escapado — el que se tapa —
> Que entre el sombrero y la capa
> Se os ve apenas la nariz? (214:28-215:2)

— he hears his announcement of Elvira's death casually brushed aside as of no importance whatever. Certainly, he is told, it is foolish to risk his life duelling "por no sé qué / Cuento de amor" (218:24-5), and if he insists on doing so he must wait while Don Félix coolly counts up his winnings. Love for a true Romantic meant everything,

both on earth and in eternity; love for Don Félix is a momentary
affair scarcely worthy of the name, and he flatly denies a basic
Romantic tenet which Musset wrote a whole play, *Carmosine*, to
illustrate:

> Se murió, no es culpa mía;
> Y admiro vuestro candor,
> Que no se mueren de amor
> Las mujeres de hoy en día. (219:15-18)

Having demonstrated in Parts II and III the qualities Espronceda
attributed to him in the early stanzas of the poem, Elvira and her
brother both destroyed by him, Don Félix strides into the final
section, which is to lead to his own physical destruction. He does
so with all the unruffled, witty aplomb of James Bond emerging
from yet another transatlantic jet. Neither uncomfortably close laser
beams nor the horrors of voodoo can disturb the twentieth-century
hero's calm for more than a second; his nineteenth-century counter-
part stirs the reader's admiration by encountering a spectre, a supernatural flaring up of the flame which lights a religious image, a
transformation of the town he knew into a phantasmagoric nightmare, the sight of his own funeral, and the full horror of the skeleton-
haunted house with its ghostly bride and her circling retinue, all
encountered with no more than an occasional involuntary twitch of
reaction:

> Al fin era hombre, y un punto temblaron
> Los nervios del hombre, y un punto temió;
> Mas pronto su antiguo vigor recobraron,
> Pronto su fiereza volvió al corazón. (236:5-8)

Even this only serves to reinforce the convincing portrayal of his
fearlessness, since it underlines the terror of the situation which
faces him and then shows his masterly control. Dismissing the sight
of his funeral procession as some devilish illusion, he strikes a typical
pose:

> Diciendo así, soltó una carcajada,
> Y las espaldas con desdén volvió:
> Se hizo el bigote, requirió la espada (237:11-13)

and launches into another attempt to persuade the veiled woman to
yield to his advances. "Firme el corazón", "tranquila audacia",
"osado", "alma de invencible vigor llena", "temerario brío",

"atrevido", "su temeridad raya en locura", "valeroso"— the adjectives and phrases characterising Don Félix and his intrepid behaviour accumulate, and Espronceda comments that anyone who can remain so unmoved before the fearsome sight of the advancing funeral party must have "de diamante el alma" (235:13). As we have seen, not even death in the terrifying circumstances of the dénouement can break his spirit.

In his strength of nerve, then, Don Félix is of the stuff of which most heroes are made. He even rouses envy in those for whom two sherries turn a flight of steps into an insuperable obstacle by his certainty, after only a moment's hesitation, that the capricious movements of streets and buildings around him cannot be the after-effects of alcohol, "que ya mil veces embriagarse en vano / En frenéticas órgias[15] intentara" (223:7-8). Throughout this final section Don Félix flaunts his defiance of both God and the devil in a growing climax of rebellion. These are his words as he first glimpses the wraith:

> Dios presume asustarme: ¡ojalá fuera,
> Dijo entre sí riendo, el diablo mismo!
> Que entonces, vive Dios, quién soy supiera
> El cornudo monarca del abismo. (223:9-12)

The theme continues throughout the chase. With unconscious dramatic irony, Don Félix assures his supposed prey that, even if she should be Satan himself, he must follow her beyond the threshold of Hell (225:18-22). Let God see them in each other's arms, he adds in lines which again foreshadow the finale (229:25). Faust, Dorian Gray, and others of their ilk defy God in making a pact with the devil, but this Spanish rebel has obviously declared an act of independence from both powers and, far from seeking the help of either, he openly challenges both on equal terms. "Y Dios y el diablo y yo nos conozcamos", he says to Elvira's ghost.

In this age that was intoxicated with revolt in Europe and the Americas, Lucifer had become a glamorous figure in literature, it will be remembered. Espronceda alludes to both in the three stanzas that sound a paean of admiring praise to his hero before the clasping skeleton arms are allowed to drag him to his death. In these lines

---

[15]The accent is printed above the "o" in the edition cited so as to maintain the hendecasyllabic metre. See *4*, p. 55, n. 21.

Don Félix is placed on a lofty pedestal:

Grandiosa, satánica figura,
Alta la frente, Montemar camina,
Espíritu sublime en su locura,
Provocando la cólera divina:
Fábrica frágil de materia impura,
El alma que la alienta y la ilumina,
Con Dios le iguala, y con osado vuelo
Se alza a su trono y le provoca a duelo.

Segundo Lucifer que se levanta
Del rayo vengador la frente herida,
Alma rebelde que el temor no espanta,
Hollada sí, pero jamás vencida:
El hombre en fin que en su ansiedad quebranta
Su límite a la cárcel de la vida,
Y a Dios llama ante él a darle cuenta,
Y descubrir su inmensidad intenta. (240:23-241:8)

And so, with this fanfare of verses which merit a place in any study of the Romantic hero, Don Félix moves off on the last lap of his pursuit, bold-eyed, a bawdy song on his jeering lips, his sword clanking its usual leitmotiv.

No one could say that the titanic enterprise he has undertaken in challenging the powers of good and evil has turned him into the usual Romantic leading man with his sombre gaze and furrowed brow. Introducing him, Espronceda promised us a jesting hero, and Don Félix lives up to this promise to his last breath. His aside, "¡Chasco sería!" (225:9), when he wonders if the mysterious shape may be some devout old woman, typifies his outlook throughout the nightmarish events. From first to last, his attitude to the veiled form is that mixture of the bantering and the forceful which has proved successful over the centuries. Like the "Burlador", Don Félix has no concern for his quarry's feelings ("Que yo he de cumplir mi anhelo / Aun a despecho de vos", 225:24-5), and is far more interested in making sure that his reputation is not sullied by any accusations that fear prevented him from running her to earth. Yet he masks the blatancy of his hunting instinct with an appearance of sarcastic suavity:

Y perdonadme, señora,
Si hay en mi empeño osadía,
Mas fuera descortesía
Dejaros sola a esta hora. (225:26-226:2)

In his dialogue with her there is a banteringly threatening note:

Con los mudos, reina mía,
Yo hago mucho y hablo poco. (228:24-5)

No more sermons, he begs the wraith when she warns him of hell-fire, for he has no intention of listening to any before Lent, and this solemnity does not suit her at all. Even the streets and buildings of Salamanca whirling around him like a gigantic kaleidoscope cannot quench his flippancy. His jesting imagination reduces the gyrating bell-towers to "mulas de alquiler, / Andando con campanillas" (233:27-8). The woman who is leading him onwards could well be the devil himself, he speculates prophetically, but this does not stop him from berating her as caustically as any foot-sore, irascible Spanish tourist might an indefatigable guide. She must be new around here, he complains sarcastically; walking on and on like this is madness; either she has lost the way, or this is walking for walking's sake (234:4-8). As for the silence with which she counters his attempts at conversation, "es la más rara locura / Que puede hallarse en mujer" (234:10-11).

His funeral he dismisses with a roar of laughter as the result of a false report, a boastful fabrication of Don Diego, newly arrived in Hell. The last words he speaks combine the music-hall comedian's attitude to women which we have already seen—admittedly his bride is not beautiful but, being dead, she will be far less tiresome than if she were alive (250:13-18)—with the same mocking imagination which had made light of the tricks played on his senses. If this is his wedding, he wants to know whether God or the devil organised the event; perhaps Lucifer himself may be his best man (250:19-22). His final stanza rings out with a flaunting splendour of defiance:

Cualquiera o entrambos con su corte toda,
Estando estos nobles espectros aquí,
No perdiera mucho viniendo a mi boda ...
Hermano don Diego, ¿no pensáis así? (250:23-6)

With this fire of spirit, this impatience with the limits of everyday existence, perhaps two or three centuries earlier an orthodox Don

Félix might even have been one of the band of Spanish religious reformers who pushed forward with the exploration of spiritual experience just as their contemporaries discovered unknown territory in South America. Elvira's ghostly shape certainly seems to lure him on less because it is female than because he quickly divines in it a metaphysical challenge. As it is, product of a revolution-shaken Europe, he diverts his frenzied energy into the pursuit of pleasure:

> La vida es la vida: cuando ella se acaba,
> Acaba con ella también el placer.
> ¿De inciertos pesares por qué hacerla esclava?
> Para mí no hay nunca mañana ni ayer.
>
> Si mañana muero, que sea en mal hora
> O en buena, cual dicen, ¿qué me importa a mí?
> Goce yo el presente, disfrute yo ahora,
> Y el diablo me lleve siquiera al morir. (230:7-14)

Suprisingly, then, for those who may think of *El estudiante de Salamanca* as a skilfully executed piece of nineteenth-century bric-à-brac, Don Félix lines up with many of the foremost twentieth-century heroes as a vociferous exponent of metaphysical revolt. As an embodiment of man's alienation, he foreshadows fictitious beings created by Malraux and Camus, though he is not agnostic. Indeed, Espronceda perhaps comes closer to André Breton, whose rejection of orthodox religion drove him for a time into an obsession with the devil. We have already seen that the first half of the nineteenth century teemed with feelings of rebellion and spiritual anguish aroused by political, scientific, and philosophical or religious upheavals. This was no less so in the Catholic stronghold of Spain. "For the Spanish writer who had become conscious of the collapse of the old world-view among the intellectual minority", writes Donald Shaw, "there was no possibility of compromise and little hope of working out his own solution in peace. The choice for him was between orthodoxy and the void" (*30*, p. 355). Don Félix not only chooses but frenetically seeks out the void. In a Spain storm-tossed politically and threatened spiritually, he symbolically hurls himself into a void formed not by the disappearance of belief, but by the rejection of supernatural powers, both good and evil. In Donald Shaw's eyes it is Espronceda who provides the most coherent expression of the Romantics' outlook on the world:

> His return from exile seems to have been accompanied by growing intellectual preoccupation. Besides the patriotic poet and the revolutionary dreaming of love and glory, a new figure appears: the seeker after truth. But as he attempts to comfort himself for the loss of the earlier illusions by making sure that the underlying metaphysical position is still sure, we see his efforts fail. In Espronceda's *Hymn to the Sun*, for example, the sun is identified with the idea of eternal duration, with all that is reliably time-defying, including by implication those ideals, beliefs and absolutes which like the sun illuminate the world. But the climax of the whole poem is a simple negation... Thus nothing is secure. (*30*, pp. 361-2)

El diablo mundo is Espronceda's pessimistic final word on the relationship between man and a harsh God, heedless of human suffering, like the deity Voltaire had portrayed as insensible to the Lisbon earthquake of 1755 (*Candide,* 1759). Don Félix has absorbed the despairing message of *El sol* and points Espronceda's last hero, Adán, to his disillusioned conclusions about the human condition.

"Almendra españolísima de todos los donjuanes" according to Antonio Machado (quoted in *15*, p.201), Don Félix is also a universally understandable hero with his rash bravura; heir of Tirso; epitome of Romanticism in some ways; and yet at the same time strangely modern in his violent revolt against the apparently tragic limits of human existence. As he sneers through the tavern scene and whirls what seems to me, in spite of the often-heard accusations about Espronceda's wordiness, his streamlined way through streets and corridors to his death, Don Félix is a compelling hero, easily able to stand comparison with the leading men of other dramatic poems of the century, with Musset's Don Paez and Byron's Childe Harold. Yet, if measured against the severest canons of literary judgment, perhaps he just fails to join the ranks of the few really outstanding fictitious characters in world literature. It is hard to put a finger on the reason for this, but perhaps it is partly because this embodiment of revolt lacks any recorded feeling of human warmth. This could also be said of Tirso's Don Juan as far as personal relationships are concerned, yet he exudes a sense of gusto and sheer enjoyment of life itself which is missing in Don Félix. It is true that an outcry of protesting despair can form great art — in Goya's *Desastres de la Guerra,* for instance; in some of the quartets where Beethoven pours out his dread of growing deafness; in Larra's final article with its paroxysm of revulsion at moribund Spain. Nor can it be said that Don Félix's attitude is a pose. There was reason enough in both Espronceda's personal history and the history of his time to account for the challenge he flings in the face of life. Nevertheless, the final impression this dry husk of rebellion leaves is that of wit and courage but also aridity. Similarly unresolved bitterness in the *Canto a Teresa* spoils for some readers what others judge to be one of the world's great love poems. Musset's *Souvenir* (1841) treats a comparable theme of passion ending in disaster, but it ends with a paean of praise for past happiness in spite of the grief which followed.

This is not to say that *El estudiante de Salamanca* itself lacks emotional intensity. Just as the hero of *Canción del pirata* expresses Espronceda's defiance of society, so Don Félix is a mouthpiece for the author's cosmic defiance. Yet he is only a partial representation of his creator, as we have already seen. When Elvira's ghost lets out a sigh of deep sadness, the poet is suddenly heard, intervening in the action to interpret the situation, just as the chorus does in the Greek theatre. This unseen other self voices an aspect of Espronceda missing from the heartless, untormented Don Félix. Just as the *Canto a Teresa* suddenly explodes in the middle of *El diablo mundo*, so here a group of stanzas provide a commentary full of deep feeling on the lines which begin:

> Del hondo del pecho profundo gemido,
> Crujido del vaso que estalla al dolor,
> Que apenas medroso lastima el oído,
> Pero que punzante rasga el corazón. (226:7-10)

In *El diablo mundo* Espronceda still hears grief as a sigh:

> Y en torno resonó triste gemido,
> Como el recuerdo que en el alma deja
> La voz de la mujer que hemos querido. (5, p. 86)

Rather than an aside, this passage in *El estudiante de Salamanca* might well be taken as the emotional crux of the poem and the key to the hero's attitude to life, for Espronceda's feelings burst from it with the force that, in his unusual image, shatters a vase.

In this exploration of his own grief, he puts into effect the Romantic belief that an artist should draw on his own life-blood of emotions and experiences for material, just as the pelican in Musset's poem draws blood from its breast to feed its young (*La Nuit de mai*, 1835). Don Félix may stride through life unmoved, but his creator in this interjection joins the ranks of those Romantics—fictitious or flesh and blood—who have often been accused of a lachrymose, self-pitying tendency to wallow in their own sorrow. The theatre of the time was full of such soliloquies as those in which Hernani (in Act I, scene 2 in Hugo's play of the same name) or Don Alvaro in the Duque de Rivas's *La fuerza del sino* (Act III, scene 3) pour out before the audience the grief which an unkind fate has inflicted upon them. This introspection can be wearisome if it is insincere or badly written, and it repels instantly readers born with a naturally stiff Anglo-Saxon upper lip. It is probably passages like this which would be quoted as examples by critics who find Espronceda wordy. Yet it might be asked whether any length could be too great to spell out intense human distress, especially when it is not purely personal but reflects the feelings of many a contemporary and many a later reader. This was, after all, a period when in Paris "l'on entendait vraiment dans la nuit craquer la détonation des pistolets solitaires", as Gautier recalled,[16] and when in Madrid Larra, wholly overwhelmed by a despair perhaps not too different from Espronceda's, finally drew his gun on himself. Even those who complain of Romantic exaggeration might concede that some of these lines in *El estudiante de Salamanca* are written with the restraint of simplicity. We read, for instance:

Y ha visto los hombres pasar en el suelo

Y nadie a sus quejas los ojos volvió. (227:5-6)

There is restraint of emotion too. The lines tell of a self-imposed mask of false gaiety which hides grief in order to keep the world's mockery at bay, concealing despair beneath stoical dignity as Vigny recommended (*La Mort du loup*, 1843). Again there is a foretaste of *Canto a Teresa*, where the penultimate stanza includes the lines:

Yo escondo con vergüenza mi quebranto,

Mi propia pena con mi risa insulto. (5, p. 102)

In fact, turned into plain everday prose of the sort Molière's Monsieur

[16]In his *Histoire du Romantisme* (Paris, 1911), p. 154 (1st edition, 1874). "You really heard the crack of solitary pistol shots during the night."

Jourdain did not know that he had been speaking, these stanzas tell
a story which must constantly pour along telephone wires into the
ears of twentieth-century Samaritans.

It is in these few stanzas too that we can perhaps look for the key
to understanding Don Félix's single-minded rebellion. Far from
unduly parading details of a personal tragedy before his readers,
Espronceda alludes to it in only the most veiled way. Nor does he
specifically refer to himself at all, but simply to someone who has
known sorrow and can therefore understand the depths of Elvira's
sigh. He speaks of happiness which had seemed as if it must be everlasting, but which had dissolved in the space of a day, leaving him
drowning in agony in a shoreless sea. He speaks of the grief which is
his constant companion, and of his sense of isolation. Both nature
and men are completely impervious to his trouble. The moon still
shines serenely, indifferent to his distress as it is to Elvira's in Part II.
By the time *El diablo mundo* was written, the moon is even thought
of as deepening human sadness:

> Allí colgada la luna
> Con torva, cárdena faz,
> Triste, fatídica, inmóvil
> En la inmensa oscuridad
> Más entristece que alumbra,
> Cual lámpara sepulcral. (*5*, p. 84)

Espronceda, if he is indeed the unnamed man he describes, adds
his contribution to the theme of isolation which was voiced so often
in the early nineteenth century—the isolation of artists from their
new public; the isolation of "exaltés" like Musset, Vigny, and Larra
from their fellow men who failed to understand them; the isolation
of many contemporaries in a universe which no longer seemed
familiar once the foundations of religion had been shaken. His
nostalgia for the past and its lost happiness is not novel; rather, it
belongs to a traditional theme which, as countless writers of today's
popular songs testify, has never passed out of fashion. Some of his
lines strike home with the force of truisms which are always being
freshly discovered:

> Y aquellos placeres, que el triste ha perdido,
> No huyeron del mundo, que en el mundo están,

> Y él vive en el mundo do siempre ha vivido,
> ¡Y aquellos placeres para él no son ya! (227:15-18)

Perhaps the most significant stanza is that which uncovers the reason for this loss of pleasure. Espronceda refers to the man "que descubre por fin la mentira" and, equally desolating for a writer who firmly stated that imagination was worth more than reason,[17] to "el que la triste realidad palpó" (227:19-20). It is left to the reader to interpret these lines as he will, applying them to the breakdown of the relationship with Teresa or to disillusionment with life as a whole, but the next two lines leave us in no doubt that it was not just a woman but the world in general that had embittered Espronceda. He refers to:

> El que el esqueleto de este mundo mira,
> Y sus falsas galas loco le arrancó... (227:21-2)

As Don Félix snatches away the bridal veil, expecting to find a beautiful woman but confronted instead by a hideous skeleton, so Espronceda looks on the horror of a dead universe where he no longer finds any beauty, once the veil of illusion has been torn away. In his *Cántico espiritual* San Juan de la Cruz personifies the soul and its God as a girl seeking her elusive beloved, then as a betrothed couple, and finally as husband and wife. It seems as if *El estudiante de Salamanca* may also be an allegory, where the author depicts his pursuit of life's beauty and then his horrific disillusionment. If so, the two lines quoted above could well stand as an epigraph for the whole dramatic poem. The last stanzas of this section expose depths of despair to equal any in Romantic literature or music. For the sufferer there is no comfort, no hope and no respite, as he lives in the past, feeding his own sorrow in the best tradition of the movement. There is a sadly prophetic note about the words "Quien haya sentido... / Al cuello cien nudos echarle el dolor" (228:3,6), since Espronceda was to die choked by diphtheria, and dabblers in current psychological theory may pause over these lines,

[17]Espronceda wrote in the prospectus to *El Siglo*: "Opuestos a las heladas doctrinas del siglo XVIII, que reduciendo al hombre moral a una máquina regida por leyes positivas y matemáticas, tienden a degradar la imaginación, y a ridiculizar las pasiones nobles del corazón humano, creemos que los sentimientos del hombre son superiores a sus intereses, sus deseos a sus necesidades, su imaginación a la realidad."

remembering the speculated relationship between the terms an individual uses to describe his emotional trouble and the physical area where illness subsequently strikes.

It is, then, this almost anonymous figure suddenly interposed in the poem who explains the despair which sends Don Félix hurtling like a hurled spear of defiance through the plot. Elvira too seems more a symbol or an embodied attitude than an individual human being, though it could reasonably be argued that a dramatic poem does not provide the space to develop more than the outline of a character. In any case Romantic writers, like opera composers, often pour from the lips of cardboard characters powerful emotions whose basic truth strikes home unerringly. Whatever an audience thinks of the conventional repertoire of cloaks, daggers, thunderstorms and sudden deaths in Verdi's *Rigoletto*, it cannot ignore the music's convincing expression of affection, anger and grief. Elvira is the vehicle through which Espronceda expresses the antithetical ecstasy and anguish of love and, as with Don Félix, the way in which she is portrayed reveals a good deal about the author himself.

The story of her life, occupying the end of Part I and the whole of Part II, is a complete narrative poem in its own right. As in a reversed "before" and "after" advertisement, we see her first before Don Félix has abandoned her; then a section describing the madness caused by his betrayal is interrupted by a passage meditating on women and love in general; finally she is shown on her death-bed (like Don Quixote, recovering her wits in her last hours), and then in her tomb. We have already seen that the passages dominated by Don Félix use a completely different colour-range–black, shot with melodramatic red and pallid flickers of light–to the delicate moonlit background against which Elvira moves and, in an antithesis which Hugo would have relished, Elvira herself is a complete foil to her lover. The villain in his black cloak and the "blanca silfa" that he betrays are the traditional couple of Romantic drama and Victorian melodrama, with black as an obvious symbol for the vice of the oppressor and white the token of his victim's virtue and innocence. Wardrobe mistresses in the Romantic period had in fact little scope to show their imagination in dressing leading ladies, since pure white was almost a uniform for heroines. Hugo's instructions incorporated in the text of his plays lay down that *Hernani*'s Doña

Sol and *Les Burgraves*'s Régina should wear white, as does the Queen in *Ruy Blas* to demonstrate that like them she is "une pure et lumineuse créature", her husband existing in name only.[18]

For a poet accused of verbosity, Espronceda shows remarkable restraint in giving us scarcely any more precise details about his heroine's appearance than about the hero's. Although these were the days of catalogue-like descriptions, we are told no more than that she is "bella", with "dulces ojos lánguidos y hermosos", and that her hair, in the mad scenes at least, flows loosely down her back (194:1-2; 196:25-6). Yet even in her madness she is a creature of beauty, seen against the poetic background of a moonlit garden. Espronceda never introduces into her portrait the images of degradation which in the *Canto a Teresa* depict a woman's beauty turned into something vile. Some readers may fuse Elvira in their mind's eye with Millais's painting of Ophelia, since the resemblance between Shakespeare's and Espronceda's descriptions of a crazed girl is unmistakable. Ophelia, the "rose of May" (*Hamlet*, IV. 5) and Elvira, whose heart opens to pleasure "como al rayo del sol rosa temprana" (194:11-12), both weave garlands of flowers, wander down to a river-bank, and sing snatches of song. In *Hamlet* the Queen relates how:

> There is a willow grows aslant a brook,
> That shows his hoar leaves in the glassy stream;
> There with fantastic garlands did she come,
> Of crow-flowers, nettles, daisies and long purples,
> That liberal shepherds give a grosser name,
> But our cold maids do dead men's fingers call them:
> There on the pendent boughs, her coronet weeds
> Clambering to hang, an envious sliver broke;
> When down her weedy trophies and herself
> Fell in the weeping brook. Her clothes spread wide;
> And mermaid-like, awhile they bore her up:
> Which time she chanted snatches of old tunes,
> As one incapable of her own distress,
> Or like a creature native and indued
> Unto that element ... (IV. 7)

[18]See *Hernani*, Act I, the stage instruction at the end of scene 1; *Les Burgraves*, Part I, the stage instruction at the end of scene 2; and *Ruy Blas*, Act II, the stage instruction at the beginning of scene 1 for the Queen's costume, and the preface to the play for the reference to her as a "pure, luminous creature".

Elvira stays on the bank, casting blossoms one by one into the water and watching their progress with a distraught eye as she sings love-songs. It is only in tears that she drowns. Earlier, as she distractedly plucks petals from flowers (196:27-8), she is again reminiscent of Ophelia handing out sprigs of rosemary, pansies, fennel, columbines, daisies and rue (IV. 5), but in his portrayal of madness Espronceda could well also have had in mind one or more of the many nineteenth-century heroines whose wits were crazed by frustrated love. Donizetti's Lucia di Lammermoor had already sung her famous mad-scene with its aria "Strew a flower on my grave". Recently published literature too provided him with similar cases: Laura in Martínez de la Rosa's *La conjuración de Venecia* (1830), for instance, and another Elvira in *El doncel de don Enrique el doliente*, Larra's novel of 1834. Probably he needed no more than his own imagination to give the reader a convincing picture of a distraught girl wandering uncertainly in the moonlight with an anxious, bemused look in her eyes. Like a film director, he shows us how she moves to and fro, now sinking down, now starting up in a panic, running across the garden, stopping to listen for the serenade that will not be heard again; murmuring endearments to the lover she momentarily thinks is still beside her, beseeching his pity, sometimes weeping, sometimes smiling in her delirium. Her cheeks are feverish with a passion that Espronceda depicts in imagery that he was to use for the same purpose in *Canto a Teresa*. Elvira's fever is:

> una ola
> Del mar que en fiera borrasca
> El viento de las pasiones
> Ha alborotado en su alma (197:9-12)

and elsewhere:

> Y su frente en revuelto remolino
> Ha enturbiado su loco pensamiento,
> Como nublo que en negro torbellino
> Encubre el cielo y amontona el viento. (200:9-12)

In the later poem the poet describes how visions from history

> A un tiempo mismo en rápida tormenta,
> Mi alma alborotaban de contino,
> Cual las olas que azota con violenta
> Cólera impetuoso torbellino. (5, p. 99)

Pictorially, then, Elvira's portrayal consists of a series of pastel cameos, which show her against an enchanting background and untouched by ugliness, even when madness intervenes. Emotionally she is just as appealing; every inch a Romantic heroine, and one of the most attractive produced by Spain. Part of her charm is the impression Espronceda gives in the "before" portrait of a youthfulness as fresh as the down on a newly hatched chicken and which makes her as defenceless as any newborn creature. An "early rose", just as Teresa is described as "sobre tallo gentil temprana rosa" (5, p. 100), Elvira naturally attracts the adjectives "inocente" and "candorosa". She is as trusting, we are told, as any baby lying at rest in its mother's arms. Naturally too she invites imagery taken from the heavens. She is a shy star, an "ángel puro de amor que amor inspira" (194:7). Purity is one of her essential characteristics, and in its light she judges everything in the world to be equally pure. The world with its magic and splendour is no more than a mirror of Teresa's beauty, writes Espronceda in *El diablo mundo*, and here he sketches the same idea:

> Del cielo azul al tachonado manto,
> Del sol radiante a la inmortal riqueza,
> Al aire, al campo, a las fragantes flores,
> Ella añade esplendor, vida y colores. (194:29-32)

Like Elvira too, Teresa before her corruption is "angélica, purísima y dichosa" (5, p. 100). If anyone has ever tried to record the number of times Romantic heroines have been described as angelic beings, it cannot have been long before his overflowing filing cabinets crowded him out of his own study. It goes without saying that "angel" is a term that has been applied to women in literature before and after the nineteenth century, and even in the more lyrical moments of flesh-and-blood courtship, but it is only too well known that the Romantic, as man and author alike, tended to put the woman he idealised not merely on a pedestal but on a heavenly plane. Espronceda was talking not to some plaster-cast heroine of fiction but to a real woman when he addressed her in *Canto a Teresa* as "astro de la mañana luminoso", "ángel de luz", and wrote:

> Aun cercaba tu frente el blanco velo
> Del serafín, y en ondas fulguroso,
> Rayos al mundo tu esplendor vertía. (5, p. 101)

Just how much of a prelude to disaster it could be to endow a fellow human being with divine qualities the latter part of the *Canto* proves. The ensuing tragedy is reflected in certain lines of *El estudiante de Salamanca* too, as we shall see.

In the meantime Espronceda established that, like almost all other Romantic heroines before fashion began to prefer the demonic type such as Carmen, Elvira combines maximum purity with maximum passion. In this she is similar to Inés, Zorrilla's novice who risks her soul to obtain the salvation of another Don Juan, it will be remembered. She may be an "ángel puro", but the full phrase reads "ángel puro de amor", and love is not meant solely in the spiritual sense. The introductory stanzas comment on her pride in her lover, the ardent thirst with which she drinks in his honeyed words. A fanatic in love, like Hugo's Doña Sol, she focuses the whole of her happiness on the man who has won her heart:

> Fueron sus ojos a los ojos de ella
> Astros de gloria, manantial de vida.
> Cuando sus labios con sus labios sella
> Cuando su voz escucha embebecida,
> Embriagada del dios que la enamora,
> Dulce le mira, extática le adora. (195:3-8)

Don Félix may not believe in love at all, but Elvira, like so many men and women in her period, treats it as a religion. It is not by accident that religious vocabulary such as the words "dios" and "adora" are used in conveying her attitude to her lover, as it was in the medieval poetry of courtly love. Espronceda refers to this state of total absorption again in *Canto a Teresa*, though there the intoxication is mutual: "Tú embriagada en mi amor, yo en tu hermosura" (*5*, p. 101).

It is not Elvira's obsession with her love –"amar como jamás amó ninguna", as she says of herself (201:6)– that causes the real-life Teresa's downfall, but the same images are used to depict their wretchedness. The petals that Elvira scatters vanish like her love affair and her hopes:

> Deshojadas y marchitas,
> ¡Pobres flores de tu alma! (198:9-10)

So with Teresa,

> Las rosas del amor se marchitaron,
> Las flores en abrojos convirtieron (*5*, p. 101)

and the "delicate flower of her beauty" is battered by the north wind of grief. This image is certainly not Espronceda's sole property. Garcilaso's sonnet "En tanto que de rosa y azucena" springs to mind as one of the best-known variations on the same theme and so obvious a metaphor must have as long a history as poetry itself. Yet Espronceda handles it with such intensity of feeling that in these two poems it becomes his leitmotiv of destroyed love and life.

The meditation on women and love which divides the mad-scene into two sections is a cloud-burst of imagery, and the concentration of metaphors reflects how deeply the subject stirred Espronceda's emotions. Like the poet's soliloquy which interrupts the action in Part IV, this is a key passage for an understanding of the author himself. Fallen leaves, rather than fallen petals, represent vanished illusions here as the wind makes them its playthings, but the first image in these lines (198:11-199:28) consists of one of those vivid touches of colour and light which are characteristic of Espronceda. Elvira is compared to a white cloud in the light of dawn, dyed with opalescent and scarlet hues, until her virginal purity disintegrates, her enchantment blown away on the breeze with the happiness love had promised her. The scene changes to compare a heart empty of love to a desert covered with sorrow's lava. Again the shutter clicks and now we find ourselves looking at a seascape – a dark wood, the sun sinking into the waves, a flock of gulls on the shore, a ship in the distance – a verbal magic lantern feeds the eyes and the imagination with enchanting sights.

Leaving the succession of images, Espronceda rounds on woman-kind with one of the most significant stanzas in the poem:

> Tú eres, mujer, un fanal
> Transparente de hermosura:
> ¡Ay de ti! si por tu mal
> Rompe el hombre en su locura
> Tu misterioso cristal. (199:14-18)

He returns to the same image in the final section in Part II where he shows Elvira on her death-bed. Dying, she is a rose withered by grief, a breath of fragrance carried away by the wind, but also:

> Vaso de bendición, ricos colores
> Reflejó en su cristal la luz del día,
> Mas la tierra empañó sus resplandores
> Y el hombre lo rompió con mano impía. (201:17-20)

Rich in its interplay of colour and light, this image is echoed later when Espronceda compares the ghostly Elvira's deeply sorrowful sigh to a shattered vase and begins his exploration into the tragedy of shattered illusions.

More important for most readers than the picturesqueness of this repeated metaphor is the light it throws on Espronceda's attitude to women as it reappears in *Canto a Teresa*. "¿Quién, impío, / ¡Ay! agostó la flor de tu pureza?" he asks Teresa. It seems as if love itself is a holy thing in his eyes, since on her death-bed he calls Elvira a "celestial soul born for love". Love was the "source of her life". "Beloved of the Lord", she died "full of love and youth" (201:22-202:4). There is no condemnation of passion itself here, rather the reverse. Even the madness brought on by betrayal is desirable, for its tortured sweetness is preferable by far to the misery of cold reason:

> Que es la razón un tormento,
> Y vale más delirar
> Sin juicio, que el sentimiento
> Cuerdamente analizar. (199:24-7)

In a way these are some of the saddest lines in the poem, since they reflect Espronceda's view that real life is intolerable. Sharing his feeling, it is small wonder that so many contemporaries plunged into escapism in one of its many forms. Elvira's end bears out that passion itself is not heinous sin in Espronceda's eyes. Love, we are told, is the cause of her death (Espronceda clearly does not share Don Félix's incredulity that such a thing could happen), and her soul is wafted straight to Heaven.

It is true that in the farewell letter she writes moments before dying she begs God's forgiveness for her "desvarío", for dwelling on the memories which still fill her with delight. But a few lines later on she admits that her heart still burns with love. Her very last words are a reminder of her despair:

> Adiós, adiós, ¡tu corazón perdí!
> — ¡Todo acabó en el mundo para mí! (204:7-8)

but the letter as a whole has a dignity made all the more human by a momentary wavering. Elvira begins by telling Don Félix that she asks neither his love nor his pity, then in the closing lines as she feels death closing in there comes a quickly stifled appeal, "Ámame: no, perdona: ¡inútil ruego!" (204:6). Above all there is a lack of bitterness

which Espronceda himself is far from achieving. She speaks
rapturously of the happiness she knew in the days when Don Félix's
words were for her an "éxtasis celestial". In contrast with the acrid
despair of the final stanzas of *Canto a Teresa* and of the poet's
soliloquy in *El estudiante de Salamanca*, Elvira says, and repeats:
"¡Dulces horas de amor, yo las bendigo!" (203:6-7).

There is generosity as well as dignity in Elvira's last message to
her seducer. If the thought of her unhappiness troubles him, she asks
no more than that he shall read her words with pity and then forget
her. Let him weep for her, she adds in words that echo Dido's in
Purcell's opera, but may her memory cause him no sorrow. Obviously
their acquaintanceship had not deepened beyond serenades and
passionate embraces, or she would not have wasted ink urging this
most callous of rakes to be free from remorse. Her generosity
becomes almost superhuman when she wishes him future pleasure,
success, happiness and even – true test of an angelic nature – the love
of other women. It could be that Elvira inherited her great-heartedness
from another forsaken woman rather than drawing it from
Espronceda's imagination, for some of the lines seem to echo Julia's
letter in Canto I of Byron's *Don Juan*, as Philip H. Churchman has
pointed out (*12*, pp. 161-3). Julia has been consigned to a convent
rather than to an early grave, but many of her sentiments are similar
to Elvira's:

> I loved, I love you, for this love have lost
> State, station, heaven, mankind's, my own esteem,
> And yet cannot regret what it hath cost,
> So dear is still the memory of that dream;
> Yet, if I name my guilt, 'tis not to boast,
> None can deem harshlier of me than I deem:
> I trace this scrawl because I cannot rest –
> I've nothing to reproach or to request. . . .
>
> You will proceed in pleasure, and in pride,
> Beloved and loving many; all is o'er
> For me on earth, except some years to hide
> My shame and sorrow deep in my heart's core:
> These I could bear, but cannot cast aside
> The passion which still rages as before, –
> And so farewell – forgive me, love me – No,
> That word is idle now – but let it go.

My breast has been all weakness, is so yet,
But still I think I can collect my mind;
My blood still rushes where my spirit's set,
As roll the waves before the settled wind;
My heart is feminine, nor can forget —
To all, except one image, madly blind;
So shakes the needle, and so stands the pole,
As vibrates my fond heart to my fix'd soul.

(CXCIII, CXCV-CXCVI)

Narciso Alonso Cortés has noticed similarities in other letters of farewell, in that which Pope imagined Heloise writing to Abelard, for instance, and in Ovid's *Heroides* (6, p. 126).

Beautiful, innocent, and absorbed solely and fatally by passion, Elvira is the quintessential Romantic heroine. What may seem puzzling is that such an idealistic, forgiving being should be transformed into an agent of vengeance, so that the writer of the noble letter of farewell becomes the spectre who leads Don Félix to his doom (admittedly uttering repeated warnings as she does so), and finally imprisons him in her skeletal arms as he sinks exhausted. Perhaps, if pressed on the point, Espronceda might have argued that the Elvira of Part IV was not the girl of the earlier canto but simply her skeleton animated by supernatural forces, just as these forces use the Commander's statue to drag Tirso's Don Juan to Hell. The same sort of transformation a few years later saw a loving village-girl in Adam's ballet *Giselle, ou les Wilis*, after broken promises had destroyed her reason and driven her to suicide, turned into a forest spirit or "wili" whose duty (successfully evaded) was to lure her former lover to dance until he died from exhaustion.

What perhaps strikes the reader most in Part II is that, judging by the imagery of the broken lantern and shattered vase (and the withered rose in *Canto a Teresa*), women in Espronceda's world seem to be in an impossible situation. We have seen that Espronceda paints in glowing colours Elvira's capacity for adoration, for responding ardently to the man who wins her affection. Yet if she allows man's "mano impía" to touch her, her filigree fragility is destroyed. It is as though woman for Espronceda is like an ethereal creature from another planet or from a rarified spirit world who cannot make contact with man, as one human being with another, and survive. If this is so it is an extreme example of the Romantic tendency to put women on a higher plane than men, and of the Romantic despair at the discovery that, once grounded, these goddesses had their full share of earthly frailties and infidelities. Espronceda's own unhappy story is matched by Larra's disastrous relationships with women – first with the child-bride whom he had loved at first sight and who appeared designed to provide him with nothing that he required from marriage; then with the "femme fatale" who helped to drive him to suicide.

The all-or-nothing attitude that sees woman as either an angel of purity or a heap of rubble, as fragile glass fragmented by man's sacrilegious hand, becomes far more disturbing in *Canto a Teresa*. Simpler though Elvira's story is, it is difficult to read Espronceda's narrative without seeing the real Teresa Mancha in her, and Part II of *El estudiante de Salamanca* as a foreshadowing of the famous Canto II of *El diablo mundo*. The earlier work presents us simply with an idealised figure of a girl whose mind and very life are destroyed by seduction and betrayal, so that it seems natural to picture her as a "fanal / Transparente de hermosura" (199:14-15) and a "vaso de bendición" reduced to splinters (201:17-20). With Teresa, however, death is preceded by a living death of degradation, described by her lover with terms of grieving loathing. The golden-winged butterfly, early rose, crystalline spring, morning star, and angel of light, are sullied and become foul; the water of love's spring is poisoned. It seems churlish to pause during the splendid flow of this poetry, but the lingering feeling persists that poor Teresa's memory is suffering from the inability to see woman other than perched high on a pedestal or lying shattered at its base. One cannot help wondering when Teresa's statue hit the ground in Espronceda's view. Was it when she was unfaithful to him by running away from the apartment where he had installed her in Madrid? If so, it cannot have been infidelity itself but infidelity to this particular love-affair that withered the rose of her purity in his eyes, since she was already breaking marriage vows when she eloped with him. The jarring note would vanish from the superb poetry if there were the least acknowledgement that the poet himself had contributed, however slightly, to the crumbling of love's ideal; perhaps in any case the discord is inaudible to a male reader's ears. It is probably unrealistic to expect that Espronceda could have shaken off an outlook so common in his age. The same dual attitude to women can be seen in Musset, who treated some (including the young girls of good family who threw themselves at him in his later years) with almost poetic delicacy and respect, and yet who was quite capable of brutality to prostitutes, throwing one downstairs in what was no doubt a fit of remorse for his own lapse.

4 *The narrative. Sources and structure*

The Biblical reminder that there is nothing new under the sun sometimes seems tailor-made to apply to the content of nineteenth-century literature. Some themes became so popular – the rebellious, cynical hero; the flower-like heroine driven to despair or distraction; moonlit or storm-racked landscapes; anything related to the supernatural world with its panoply of spectres, tombs and skeletons; the exotic poetry of the torrid South or the gothic North – that they were in constant use throughout the Romantic period. Trying to solve the cat's cradle of possible sources and influences has kept scholars busy ever since. Every major writer's output has been examined minutely in an attempt to discover which works he had read and which might have lingered in his subconscious mind, just as an owl's pellets are put under the microscope by ornithologists intent on discovering its diet. So involved does the process become that the only consolation is to think of some twenty-first-century academic trying to work out which bedroom scene was the source for which others in twentieth-century films and television plays. It is scarcely surprising that the study of authors' possible debts to each other has led to the well-known debates as to whether Espronceda and Musset were mere satellites of Byron or independent artists who simply reflected similar personalities and the same European state of mind at this period (as did Leopardi). Musset certainly had his answer for what he regarded as an unfounded belittling of his originality:

> Mon verre n'est pas grand,
> Mais je bois dans mon verre.[19]

Sometimes frustrating because of its uncertainties, the search for works which Espronceda had read and which may have helped to shape *El estudiante de Salamanca* can nevertheless be illuminating. There are perhaps three categories to be considered: literature or legends to which he refers himself or which resemble parts of his

---

[19]*La Coupe et les lèvres*, Dédicace à M. Alfred Tattet. "My glass is small, but it is from that alone that I drink."

dramatic poem so closely that only direct influence or the greatest coincidence could account for their similarity; texts by authors whom Espronceda is known to have read or very likely did so since, for instance, the writer was one of his friends; literature which was popular at the time and which Espronceda might have known. The first category includes the theme of the Dance of Death, Elvira's madness and the letter she wrote in the sane moments before she died, and Don Félix's relationship to the Don Juan legend. These topics have already been touched on but, as an illustration of the complex history of some of Espronceda's themes, let us look first at the incident in which Don Félix witnesses his own funeral, then at the appearance of the dead, and finally at the transformation of a beautiful woman into a skeleton. An exhaustive survey of the sources for these episodes can be found in Robert Marrast's study of the poem (*16*, pp. 647-60).

Small wonder that the scene in which a man finds himself confronting his own coffin should have recurred in nineteenth-century literature, since this is precisely the type of lugubrious situation which the Romantics relished. Not only Espronceda but Zorrilla (*El capitán Montoya*, 1840, and *Don Juan Tenorio*, 1844), García de Villalta (*El golpe en vago*, 1835), and Mérimée (*Les Ames du purgatoire*, 1834) are among the authors who drew on the theme during this period. Marrast points out one of the earliest versions, which told the tale of a young student, Lisardo, whose story was well known to the nineteenth-century public, although it often confused him with the *Burlador de Sevilla*'s hero. The legend is thought to have been current in Spain before 1570, but in that year it was published by Antonio de Torquemada in his *Jardín de flores curiosas*. A young man about to creep into a convent to visit a nun whom he loves sees his own funeral service taking place in a chapel. Returning home, he is torn to pieces by two Hound of the Baskervilles-type black dogs which have followed him. Other versions found their way into print. One by Cristóbal Bravo in verse was published in 1572, and in 1658 Cristóbal Lozano's *Soledades de la vida y desengaños del mundo* appeared. Whether or not Espronceda knew any of these early presentations of the legend, it is highly probable that he had read one whose plot mirrors that of *El estudiante de Salamanca* more closely.

Several years before Espronceda produced the first section of his work, Agustín Durán had published a two-part ballad under the title of *Lisardo el estudiante de Córdoba*.[20] Durán relates that the public was already familiar with the substance of these two *romances*, with their tale of the young student at Salamanca who asks for the hand in marriage of Teodora, sister of a university friend, only to be told that she is to become a nun. Teodora herself rejects his advances and as he leaves her house he hears one of the sounds with which *El estudiante de Salamanca* opens – the clash of sword blades. He follows a mysterious *embozado* who leads him on a rapid journey through the city – a very much scaled-down form of Don Félix's pursuit of the spectre, and without the phantasmagoric transformation of streets and buildings. Outside the city they reach, as Don Félix does, a horrific ruin and the cloaked figure warns Lisardo that a man is to be killed there. His parting advice that Lisardo should reform his ways is more effective than the spectre's warnings to Don Félix, and the student falls unconscious.

At the opening of the second ballad, we see him being tempted by Teodora who, annoyingly, has changed her mind about her vocation. Here he is certainly unlike Don Félix who, rushing determinedly to his destruction, cannot claim any sympathy for having been led astray by the woman he pursues. At midnight, the most crowded hour in the Romantic day, Lisardo is on his way to carry off the reluctant nun when he hears shouts of "Si es don Lisardo, matadle", followed by the sound of sword-play and a cry which again reminds us of the beginning of *El estudiante de Salamanca*: "¡Ay que me han muerto!" A corpse falls at his feet. Then, like Don Félix, he sees a funeral procession approaching and learns that the body in the coffin is his own. From this point the two plots diverge, but clearly the similarities suggest that Espronceda had read or heard the ballads and remembered several striking situations when he came to write his own work. To say this does not diminish his stature in any way since he builds around the framework taken from the ballads a whole new fabric, atmospheric and impressionistic, before incorporating it into the larger structure of his poem. Benito Varela Jácome

[20]Nos 1271-2 in *Romancero general*, II, Biblioteca de Autores Españoles, XVI (Madrid, 1851, reprinted 1926), pp.264-8.

believes that García de Villalta's novel *El golpe en vago* was probably an even stronger influence on Espronceda (*4*, p. 15, and see also *25*). The protagonist here thinks that he is watching his own funeral, but when he follows an *embozado* out of the city, he learns that the dead man simply bore the same name as his own.

Robert Marrast also draws attention to the number of works which show spectres uttering warnings to the living, as Elvira's ghost does to Don Félix, or leading them to their doom. Some of these recall *El burlador de Sevilla*. In *La constante cordobesa (Historias peregrinas y ejemplares*, Saragossa, 1623), for instance, Gonzalo de Céspedes y Meneses shows a dead father rising from beneath his tomb-stone to frighten off his married daughter's would-be lover. In another of Céspedes y Meneses's works the resemblance to *El estudiante de Salamanca* is much closer. The hero of *Varia fortuna del soldado Píndaro* (Lisbon, 1626) has killed a French aristocrat in a duel. Later in Granada he tracks a veiled woman through a maze of streets which always seem to lead towards a cemetery. The interior of the house to which he is finally led is suddenly transformed into a room where stands a coffin draped in black. From it the blood-stained corpse of the French baron rises to continue the duel.

Yet another macabre touch in Don Félix's story, the name of the sepulchrally dark calle del Ataúd, was almost certainly gleaned from the real-life story of Miguel de Mañara, a seventeenth-century superior of a religious brotherhood who had been converted by the type of alarming experience which failed to make any impression on Don Félix, and which happened to him "yendo una noche por la calle que llaman del Ataúd, en esta ciudad de Sevilla". After being knocked to the ground by a blow on the head, he heard a voice saying "Traigan el ataúd, que ya está muerto".[21] Recovering to find himself neither dead nor buried alive, he lived an exemplary life and provided a dramatic legend which attracted Mérimée among other authors. Marrast mounts a convincing case to show that Espronceda may well have known the version Mérimée gives in *Les Ames du purgatoire* as well as Spanish sources – an interesting example of literary cross-fertilisation between France and Spain. He makes his

[21]Narciso Alonso Cortés, *Zorrilla. Su vida y sus obras*, 2nd edition (Valladolid: Santarén, 1943), p. 236.

claim modestly: "On ne peut affirmer que le récit de Mérimée constitue à proprement parler une source de *El Estudiante de Salamanca*; disons seulement que notre poète l'avait sans doute lu" (*16*, p. 652).[22] Nevertheless he draws close parallels between the two texts: the heroes share the same personality; Marana (sic) and García in *Les Ames du purgatoire* wager their mistresses as Don Félix does; the funeral incident recurs; and Marana kills the brother of Fausta and Teresa in a duel. As we have seen, other works also foreshadow *El estudiante de Salamanca*, as far as certain characters and incidents are concerned. What seems significant is that Mérimée — uncharacteristically, since he prided himself on his accurate Spanish — wrote "Marana" for "Mañara", and that it was this mangled French form of the name Espronceda adopted when he introduced his hero in the first publication of Part I as "nuevo don Juan de Marana" (*Museo Artístico y Literario*, no. 4, 22 June 1837). When the 1840 edition appeared, Don Félix had become the "segundo don Juan Tenorio" with whom modern readers are familiar.

Since it seems highly probable that Espronceda read Mérimée, it is tempting to speculate which other French works he might have known and which might have lingered in his mind while he was composing his poem. Apart from the Spanish and French texts Marrast mentions, Balzac was among the many writers who handled the Don Juan theme. *L'Elixir de longue vie* (1830) is totally different from *El estudiante de Salamanca* but it too includes a funeral with a macabre touch — the dead man's head utters an eerie cry that pierces through the sounds of the organ and the choir. Nodier too comes to mind with his *Inès de las Sierras* (1837). The Spanish castle where the legend is set clearly comes from the same gothic novel tradition as the opening of Espronceda's work. As French visitors arrive, a flash of dazzling lightning tears through the sky, revealing the castle walls and the turrets "huddled like a horde of spectres". Creaking doors, owls, ruins, howling winds — most of the traditional elements of horror are there, and Inès invites Sergy to follow her down interminable dark corridors to an underground floor before she disappears

[22]"It cannot be positively stated that Mérimée's account constitutes, strictly speaking, a source of *El estudiante de Salamanca*; let us just say that our poet had probably read it."

with a shriek of terrifying laughter.

Whether or not Espronceda had come across Balzac and Nodier, he must have known of a writer as currently popular as Dumas, and Carlos Beceiro, introducing his 1965 edition of *El estudiante de Salamanca*, points out a number of similarities between the plot and that of Dumas's rip-roaring drama *Don Juan de Marana, ou la Chute d'un ange*. First staged in 1836, the play was translated into Spanish by 1838 when it was published in Tarragona, and García Gutiérrez's adaptation was staged in Madrid in 1839. This is an example of the tangled web that scholars studying influences have to unravel, since Dumas seems to have profited from his reading of Mérimée's variation on the Don Juan theme. It has been suggested that it may even have been to avoid having his Don Félix identified too much with Dumas's hero that Espronceda changed his "nuevo don Juan de Marana" into "segundo don Juan Tenorio".

Even minor touches, such as the flickering lamp on the wall of the calle del Ataúd, have been compared with details in earlier works. In *San Franco de Sena* (1654), Moreto puts on stage a young man guilty of murder and seduction who, passing through a town, tries to blow out the lamp illuminating a cross painted on a house wall. He hears the rattle of chains and a cry of " ¡Ay!" As he tries again to put out the light, a mysterious arm seizes him and he hears a warning voice. The other main theme, however, is that of the veiled woman who reveals herself to be a skeleton, and this has a long pedigree in history and fiction. A similar encounter was reported to have been experienced by a canon of Seville cathedral, although it was later sometimes added to Miguel de Mañara's story, and a good number of Golden Age plays incorporate such incidents.[23]

Such a subject is bound to grip the attention in any century, but no motif could symbolise more aptly the Romantic obsession with the antithesis between beauty and horror and, while Golden Age dramatists may introduce the girl become skeleton into their works, the nineteenth century tends to linger lovingly on every repulsive detail that can be mustered, as Espronceda does in his nauseatingly graphic description of the bride who clutches Don Félix to her.

---

[23]For instance, Calderón de la Barca, *El mágico prodigioso*; Mira de Amescua, *El esclavo del demonio*; Moreto, Cáncer and Matos Fragoso, *Caer para levantar*.

Byron, Shakespeare, Goethe, Mérimée, a host of Spanish writers and legends – these very likely furnished Espronceda's mind as he worked on *El estudiante de Salamanca*. Some debts are obvious, while there are no doubt others of which he was unaware, as memories of things read or heard rose to the surface of his mind and mingled with what he imagined. When run-of-the-mill authors at this period tackle themes as fashionable as lovelorn heroines, swash-buckling heroes, violent death and the supernatural at its most macabre, the result is a blatant patchwork of material cobbled together from easily identifiable sources, so that one is reminded of C. Day Lewis's "Do not pick the daffodils! Property of W. Wordsworth" (*The Poetic Image*, 1947, p.15). It is a measure of Espronceda's brilliance that, just as happens in Hugo's *Hernani* and *Ruy Blas*, he takes over much-handled themes and imprints his own seal on them. The study of the sources of such works is interesting but it fades from the mind as the reader becomes immersed in the text itself.

Brilliance is a term that might well be applied to the way in which Espronceda constructs his dramatic poem from the material which he has gathered or created. Although Hugo argues that the play is the most suitable literary form for the literature of his age, with hindsight it seems that the narrative poem is perhaps an especially well adapted vehicle for Romanticism, whose plays in practice tend to be more poetic than dramatic, more lyrical than skilled at exploring the realities of human nature. There is no need for a reminder that Byron had already written not only *Don Juan* but *Mazeppa* and *Childe Harold*. In France Musset made a brilliant début with *Don Paez*, *Portia* and *Les Marrons du feu*, while Hugo was to fill three series of *La Légende des siècles* with his stories in verse. On home territory, the Duque de Rivas had already composed some of his *Romances históricos*, thought to have been written mostly between 1833 and 1839.

Whereas the majority of these poems tell their tales in straight-forward fashion, relating the events they describe in chronological order, Espronceda again foreshadows modern trends by using the flash-back technique. Almost nightly nowadays audiences see this formula at work on the television screen, as well as in the theatre and cinema. Novel-readers too grapple with the complexities of the stream of consciousness. As far as Spanish literature is concerned, no one who has come to terms with Delibes's experiments in *Parábola del náufrago* or even *Cinco horas con Mario* should have any difficulty in unravelling the plot of *El estudiante de Salamanca*, and yet first-time readers sometimes complain that the thread is difficult to grasp. At least one controversy has arisen from Espronceda's juggling with time. Robert Marrast takes the duel half-heard in the opening stanza as being a different incident from the killing of Don Diego which opens Part IV, instead of a preview of it (*16*, pp. 667-8). No one but the author himself could pronounce finally on this interpretation, but is it perhaps unlikely that he would have introduced an extraneous situation into the story-line?

If we presume for a moment that Espronceda did in fact risk confusing his readers by plunging them into the midst of the action instead of opening with the exposition, he must have had good reasons for doing so, and these become clear if we re-arrange the stanzas and compare the chronological order with the more intricate one. If Espronceda had moved without interruption from the start of his tale to its end, as Keats does in *The Eve of St Agnes*, he would have given us firstly the character-sketch of Don Félix, leading into Elvira's story and followed, as in the published version, by the gambling scene, the duel in the darkness, the chase and the skeleton dance. Simply by transposing the last moments of the duel to the beginning of the poem, he gains several advantages. The most important of these is the advantage of arresting the reader's attention immediately with a gripping, mysterious opening which is far more likely to keep his eyes on the page than a routine exposition with a straightforward introduction to the main characters. It is an indication of the powerfully dramatic nature of the work that sometimes the word "play" rather than "poem" slips out when writing or talking about *El estudiante de Salamanca*, though the resources of the cinema rather than the theatre would be needed to cope with its phantasmagorias. It might be that the midnight scene in the calle del Ataúd comes first, not for any carefully worked-out reasons, but purely because it flashed into Espronceda's imagination and there sparked off the rest of the narrative. Whether the effect is calculated or created instinctively, the plot gains suspense because the reader, intrigued by the duel indicated in the opening lines, is kept waiting to find out who the duellists were and what their quarrel was.

There are critics who justify the construction of the poem by comparing it to set musical forms. Casalduero believes that it follows a symphonic logic: "las dos melodías — lírico-melancólica (femenina) y dramática (masculina) — se introducen en la primera parte, que es una obertura, teniendo como fondo el paisaje y la acción de terror" (*9*, p. 205). The two melodies meet again in Part IV and mingle in a counterpoint, once more against a background of horror. This description certainly brings home the similarity between *El estudiante de Salamanca* and Berlioz' *Symphonie fantastique* with the clanging church bells and thundering "Dies irae" of its final passage. On a smaller scale, Espronceda's poem has been compared to sonata form, and it might be added that, just as the slow movement of a sonata can throw into relief a dramatic first movement and a final "allegro" or "presto", so the lyrical interlude of Elvira's grief heightens with its contrast the effect of the work's arresting opening and the ever-growing whirlwind of its last part. It is on some commentators' misunderstanding of Casalduero's remarks that Marrast blames what is for him the mistaken view that Part I begins with a flash-back. Yet there are readers (including myself) who, approaching the text for the first time before they are aware of critical theories, simply interpret what is happening in this way. Whichever side Espronceda would declare the winner, the debate has its merits since it stimulates interest in a plot constructed with vigour, vitality and skill.

5 Conclusion

After listing the seven characteristics which could be labelled "romantic", C.S. Lewis points out that many authors qualify for the label on more than one count, and mentions several who can be included in two of his seven catagories. It is interesting to see that *El estudiante de Salamanca* contains not two but every one (in my opinion) of the Romantic elements mentioned. Perhaps it is all the more significant that the description of Romanticism with which it tallies so completely is not the brain-child of a Hispanist whose ideas have been nurtured by the works of Rivas, Larra and Espronceda himself, but of a scholar who, while he ranged over all literature, was an English specialist. This dramatic poem, then, is not only Romantic in the sense of belonging to a certain period in the nineteenth century, but also "romantic" in the timeless sense which can apply to Malory and Michelangelo, to D.H. Lawrence and Proust. If we review the seven characteristics, it is certainly a story about dangerous adventure, and qualifies even more to be called "romantic" because the adventure is set in the past of "antiguas historias". Just as certainly it includes the marvellous in the shape of the ghosts of Elvira and her brother, as well as the troop of skeletons. As far as dealing with titanic charcters and emotions is concerned, modern critics have stressed what a towering figure Don Félix is, the sort of Prometheus (though in search of women rather than fire) whom Espronceda seems to describe in *A Jarifa en una orgia*:

> Que así castiga Dios el alma osada,
> Que aspira loca, en su delirio insano,
> De la verdad para el mortal velada
> A descubrir el insondable arcano. (stanza 17)

No one would reject the adjective "macabre", C.S. Lewis's fourth point, applied to the events which take place and, as for Egoism and Subjectivism, it will be remembered that Casalduero categorises Don Félix as the "trascendentalización del yo" (*9*, pp.172-3). On the next to the last count — revolt against existing civilisation and conventions — Don Félix, even more than most Don Juans perhaps, is hell-bent on flouting society in its sexual, social and religious norms. The last criterion, that of showing a "solemn and enthusiastic" sensibility to nature, is the one which some critics, Carnero among them (*8*, p. 46), would deny as one of Espronceda's assets, and here the reader must make up his own mind whether Elvira's moonlit garden meets the requirements.

The epitome of nineteenth-century Romanticism and of more universal romantic tendencies, *El estudiante de Salamanca* has been shown to have roots fed by many sources. Because it is a great work, a knowledge of these sources can be illuminating but cannot diminish the author's achievement and originality. Supremely Romantic, it also looks forward to *modernismo* and to twentieth-century artistic techniques in general. In its material and attitudes it is both European and profoundly Spanish. Perhaps the main impression it leaves on the mind is that of brilliance and bleakness. The brilliance confronts our own era, which tends to mistrust crafts-manship in the arts, with a virtuoso display of technique. Espronceda's ability to give a sparkling performance and the type of effects he obtains prompted Carnero to compare his style to a brass band at full blast in the town square, and to add that "la banda de música de la Milicia Nacional que acompañó su cortejo fúnebre con previsibles bombos y platillos, fue una alegoría del estilo del muerto" (*8*, p.64). Perhaps a more apt comparison might be to a full orchestra playing Liszt or Berlioz (to be fair, Carnero also describes some of Espronceda's writing as "Wagnerian"), since he has at his finger-tips not only sheer power but a whole range of subtle sounds. He knows how to use the verbal equivalents of lyrical or eerie strings and woodwind instruments as well as the clatter of percussion and the din of the brass.

El estudiante de Salamanca has passionate feeling as well as technical power, but, apart from Elvira's grief, it is to be found only in the author-commentator's despair. Don Félix himself has attractive qualities, but no human warmth. Yet one feels that Espronceda's sympathy and approval are with him to the end. As the curtain falls on *El burlador de Sevilla* there is probably little doubt among the audience that, likeable rogue though he may seem to some, Don Juan has received his just deserts and that such was his creator's intention. Some critics have seen Don Félix's death as the same sort of moral judgment (*26*, p. 205), but it is difficult not to feel that, though his physical strength may fail him, he is meant to go out in a blaze of glory as a spirit that challenges the whole of a hostile universe, almost unflinchingly, and refuses to be cowed by the worst that it can do.

The bleak atmosphere surrounding Don Félix rises partly from his disregard for the fellow human beings with whom he is shown in contact, both male and female. Don Diego is dispatched with the off-hand manner of someone carving the Sunday roast and Elvira's death is a matter of complete unconcern, as we saw. "Huye, mujer; te detesto", writes Espronceda in *A Jarifa en una orgía*, continuing very much in the vein of Kingsley Amis's novel *Jake's Thing* (1978):

> Vuestros besos son mentira,
> Mentira vuestra ternura.
> Es fealdad vuestra hermosura,
> Vuestro gozo es padecer. (stanza 4)

In just this way Elvira turns into an object of ugliness and menace. Perhaps Espronceda already had the grasp of the bride-skeleton in mind when he wrote *A Jarifa* for, after proclaiming his hatred of woman, he goes on:

> Siento tu mano en la mía,
> Y tu mano siento fría,
> Y tus besos hielos son. (stanza 3)

Not only women but all earthly pleasures had lost their savour for the man who wrote these lines, and the same sort of aridity of outlook prevails in *El estudiante de Salamanca*. Don Félix may still pursue unknown beauties but, as we have seen, it seems more likely that pride drives him onwards rather than lust. If everything on earth has palled, there is nothing in Heaven that offers comfort. Espronceda sums up his view on the universe in his sonnet of dedication to the *Poesías líricas*:

> Los ojos vuelvo en incesante anhelo,
> Y gira en torno indiferente el mundo,
> Y en torno gira indiferente el cielo.
>
> (*A . . . dedicándole estas poesías*)

All that is left for Don Félix is to keep his personal integrity intact by maintaining, a century before the Existentialists, an attitude of titanic defiance to every power that exists. Physically at least, his gesture is bound to end in defeat. Small wonder that, if we interpret Don Félix's attitude as a partial reflection of Espronceda's (an interpretation which other poems confirm), the sensuous richness of *El estudiante de Salamanca* is countered by an overriding note of barrenness and despair. At one level the work is a cleverly told ghost story; at another, a dazzling display of verbal and metrical fireworks; perhaps most of all it is a portrait, not so much of "homo eroticus", as of man in rebellion against the human condition.

Appendix: Espronceda the craftsman in "polimetría"

It is a temptation to talk glibly about the effects Espronceda obtains through his use of different verse forms without examining the versification in sufficient detail to appreciate fully the variety to be found in *El estudiante de Salamanca*. Navarro Tomás has calculated that "se registran en *El estudiante de Salamanca* once metros distintos, desde dos a doce sílabas, los cuales se combinan en siete tipos de estrofas y dan lugar a cincuenta y nueve cambios métricos" (*32*, p. 392, n. 31). However much our own free-wheeling age mistrusts the rules and regulations of set metres and rhyming schemes, no one can fail to admire the sheer dexterity of those who can handle complex systems such as the Welsh *cynghanedd* with its intricate patterns of assonance or the range of Spanish metrical variations used here. When the brilliant versifier is also a true poet, as Espronceda is, then the combination of technique and artistry reaches the same heights as Liszt's music. After his apprenticeship in the Academia del Mirto, under Lista's guidance, he was well equipped to manipulate metres and, whether or not he was an innovator, as some have claimed, he must surely rank high, on technical grounds alone, among Spanish writers of poetry.

Analysis shows the following results:

Part I

189:6-190:29, "Era más de media noche" to "Pronuncia el último a Dios":
ballad metre. Octosyllabic lines with assonance in alternate (even) lines.

190:30-191:11, "El ruido" to "Se perdió":
a series of trisyllabic and tetrasyllabic lines among which are effectively interposed two lines of two syllables each — "Cesó" and "Pasó" (190:31 and 33). Navarro Tomás comments that "El rápido movimiento de los versos y la impresión de la rima aguda y oscura subrayan la temerosa escena de cuchilladas y sombras del principio de *El estudiante de Salamanca*" (*32*, p. 394).

191:12-23, "Una calle estrecha y alta" to "Al pasar frente a la cruz":

a return to ballad metre.

191:24-192:16, "Cual suele la luna tras lóbrega nube" to "Osado a su encuentro despacio avanzó":
cuartetos of dodecasyllables. The rhyme scheme is abab.

192:17-193:28, "Segundo don Juan Tenorio" to "Don Félix de Montemar":
octavillas agudas, that is: eight lines of eight syllables each. The rhyme scheme is that used most often in this stanza form: abbc deec.

194:1-195:8, "Bella y más pura que el azul del cielo" to "Dulce le mira, extática le adora":
octavas reales, that is: eight lines of eight syllables with the rhyme scheme of abababcc.

Part II

195:13-198:8, "Está la noche serena" to "Tu ilusión y tu esperanza":
octosyllabic *cuartetos* with the scheme abcb.

198:9-10, "Deshojadas y marchitas / ¡Pobres flores de tu alma!":
the section trails off, like the drooping flowers it refers to, with an octosyllabic couplet.

198:11-199:28, "Blanca nube de la aurora" to "Fijo en él el pensamiento":
quintillas, that is: stanzas of five lines with eight syllables each. The most usual rhyme scheme for *quintillas* is said to be abaab, but Espronceda constantly rings the changes; and the nine stanzas are as follows: abaab, ababa, abaab, ababa, abbab, abaab, ababa, abbab, ababa.

200:1-202:18, "Vedla, allí va que sueña en su locura" to "Moribunda su víctima escribió":
hendecasyllabic *cuartetos*: abab.

202:19-204:8, "Voy a morir: perdona si mi acento" to "¡Todo acabó en el mundo para mí!":
octavas reales (eight lines, each of eleven syllables; abababcc).

204:9-24, "Así escribió su triste despedida" to "Baña su tumba en paz su último rayo":
hendecasyllabic *cuartetos* (abab).

Part III

205:12-206:8,   "En derredor de una mesa" to "Con sus alas al pasar":
ballad form, with octosyllabic *cuartetos* and assonance.

206:11-207:14,   scene 1:
redondillas (groups of four octosyllabic lines). This is the *redondilla de rimas abrazadas*: abba.

207:16-214:5,   scene 2:
the *redondillas* continue.

214:7-26,   scene 3, "Pálido el rostro, cejijunto el ceño" to "Fijos en él los suyos, sonrió":
five hendecasyllabic *cuartetos* (abab) are used for Don Diego's entrance. Note the heavier effect.

214:28-220:14,   scene 3, continued and scene 4:
Espronceda returns to *redondillas*, except for one *décima espinela*. This is a stanza of ten lines, with the rhyme scheme abbaaccddc and an obligatory break in the sense after the fourth line. See 215:20-216:2.

Part IV

221:14-225:4,   "Vedle, don Félix es espada en mano" to "Mientras la rechaza la adusta razón":
serventesios (abab), with the *cuartetos* consisting at first of hendecasyllabic and then of dodecasyllabic lines.

225:6-226:6,   " '¡Qué! ¿sin respuesta me deja?' " to " 'Que no he seguido a una dama' ":
Don Félix first addresses the ghost in *redondillas cruzadas* (abab) and *abrazadas* (abba).

226:7-228:14,   "Del hondo del pecho profundo gemido" to "Hubiera pesado su inmenso valor":
dodecasyllabic *serventesios* (abab).

228:16-25,   " 'Si buscáis algún ingrato' " to " 'Yo hago mucho y hablo poco' ":
quintillas (abaab), for Don Félix addressing Elvira for the second time.

228:26-230:18,   "Segunda vez importunada en tanto" to "Siente don Félix y camina en pos":
dodecasyllabic *serventesios* (the first is abba, then the pattern becomes abab).

230:19-231:8,   "Cruzan tristes calles" to "Bramando Aquilón":
a passage consisting of nineteen lines in one stanza
in the form of a *silva libre*, the hexasyllabic lines
rhyming freely.

231:9-233:13,   "Y una calle y otra cruzan" to "Ella delante, él
detrás":
ballad form

233:14-234:13,   " '¡Vive Dios! dice entre sí' " to " 'Por su paso de
andadura' ":
quintillas (abaab) for Don Félix's monologue.

234:14-236:8,   "En tanto don Félix a tientas seguía" to "Pronto su
fiereza volvió al corazón":
dodecasyllabic *serventesios*.

236:9-237:10,   "– Lo que es, dijo, por Pastrana" to "Contando
que me mató –":
quintillas for Don Félix's monologue and dialogue.

237:11-239:4,   "Diciendo así, soltó una carcajada" to "Camina en
pos con decidida calma":
one   stanza,   a   hendecasyllabic   *serventesio*,
introduces an interjected fragment of narrative,
and is followed by a return to *quintillas* to record
dialogue. Then Espronceda continues the narrative
with hendecasyllabic *serventesios* once more.

239:5-244:22,   "Y la dama a una puerta se paró" to "Así la habló
con animoso acento":
octavas reales.

244:23-245:12,   " 'Diablo, mujer o visión' " to " 'Esta aventura al
extremo' ":
Don Félix speaks again to the spectre in *quintillas*.

245:13-249:4,   "Fúnebre" to "Inclinaron, formando enredor":
the dance begins and a gradual crescendo of sound
builds up. The stanzas are formed as follows:
    five lines of two or three syllables,
    nine lines of four syllables,
    fifteen lines, mostly of five syllables,
    twenty-five lines, mostly of six syllables,
    eight lines of seven syllables,
    twenty-two lines of eight syllables,
    sixteen lines of nine syllables,
    sixteen lines of ten syllables.

249:5-251:4,   "Y entonces la visión del blanco velo" to "Al Dios
por quien jura capaz de arrastrar":

	a plateau of *serventesios* for the narration of the wedding.
251:5-253:24,	"El carïado, lívido esqueleto" to "Comienza a desmayar": *octavas* of eleven, ten and nine syllables (abbc deec) are followed by *octavillas* of eight and seven syllables as the sound of the dance begins to die down.
253:25-254:22,	"Y siente un confuso" to "Desfallecer": the next twenty-eight lines are printed either in two stanzas of eight lines (continuing the *octavillas*) and two stanzas of six lines, or in one stanza. The lines gradually decrease to a tetrasyllable.
254:23-255:11,	"Y vio luego" to "Son": the first sixteen lines of this passage are printed either in one stanza or in two stanzas of eight lines each. The number of syllables decreases until the poem reaches what Janet H. Perry in the *Harrap Anthology of Spanish Poetry* (1953) calls the "final gasp" of three disyllables, to end in a monosyllable.
255:12-256:6,	"En tanto en nubes de carmín y grana" to the end: three stanzas of classic hendecasyllables bring the reader back to the normality of day-time in the city.

Bibliographical note

EDITIONS

1. The edition used here— *Espronceda. Poesías. El estudiante de Salamanca* (Madrid, 1923, reprinted 1971) – is no. 47 in the Clásicos Castellanos series. It has a thorough introduction and notes by José Moreno Villa.

2. The text can also be found in the Colección Austral, no. 917: *Poesías líricas. El estudiante de Salamanca* (Buenos Aires, 1949).

3. Carlos Beceiro's edition (Madrid: Aguilar, 1965) has an introduction which makes interesting comparisons with Dumas's play on the Don Juan theme.

4. The edition by Benito Varela Jácome in Biblioteca Anaya (no. 71) of *El estudiante de Salamanca* by itself has a valuable, very concise introduction and a bibliography (Salamanca, 1966).

5. Quotations from *Canto a Teresa* are taken from *Obras completas de Don José de Espronceda*, ed. Jorge Campos, Biblioteca de Autores Españoles, LXXII (Madrid, 1954). The introduction is well worth consulting.

BIOGRAPHICAL AND CRITICAL STUDIES

6. Alonso Cortés, Narciso, *Espronceda. Ilustraciones biográficas y críticas*, 2nd edition (Valladolid: Librería Santarén, 1945). Written at the time of the centenary of Espronceda's death with the aim of clearing up mistaken ideas about the man and the poet. Defends his character, and his originality and genius as a writer. Interesting plates showing contemporaries such as Lista.

7. Brereton, Geoffrey, *Quelques précisions sur les sources d'Espronceda* (Paris: Jouve, 1933). A study with a high reputation. The eight pages dealing with *El estudiante de Salamanca* (pp. 98-105) are packed with information and ideas.

8. Carnero, Guillermo, *Espronceda*, Colección Los Poetas (Madrid, 1974). A stimulating work. Pays particular attention to the development of Espronceda's use of language, showing how it leads to *modernismo*.

9. Casalduero, Joaquín, *Espronceda*, Biblioteca Románica Hispánica. II: Estudios y Ensayos, 49 (Madrid: Gredos, 1961). An impressive study of the author's life and writings, set against a background of the period in which he lived.

10. Cascales Muñoz, José, *D. José de Espronceda. Su época, su vida y sus obras* (Madrid: Biblioteca Hispania, 1914). An appreciative study of Espronceda as a poet and as a man who typified his time. Cascales Muñoz maintains that his personal life did not justify the legend which sprang up

about him. Interesting documents reproduced in the appendix.

11. Černy, Václav, *Essai sur le titanisme dans la poésie romantique occidentale entre 1815 et 1850* (Prague: Orbis, 1935). Useful for anyone wanting to make a comparative study of Don Félix and his contemporaries.

12. Churchman, Philip H., 'Byron and Espronceda', *Revue Hispanique*, XX (1909), 5-210. A detailed exposition of the case for Espronceda's having borrowed from Byron.

13. Cortón, Antonio, *Espronceda*, Autores célebres (Madrid, 1906). Faulted by Robert Marrast on some biographical details.

14. Gallina, Anna Maria, 'Su alcune fonti dell'*Estudiante de Salamanca*', *Quaderni Ibero-Americani* (Turin), 45-6 (1976), 231-40. The most recent synopsis of opinion on Espronceda's sources.

15. García Lorca, Francisco, 'Espronceda y el Paraíso', *The Romanic Review*, XLIII (1952), 198-204. Well worth reading for its view of Espronceda's attitude towards his female characters.

16. Marrast, Robert, *José de Espronceda et son temps. Littérature, société, politique au temps du romantisme*, Témoins de l'Espagne, série historique, III (Paris, 1974). An indispensable work which brings a vast amount of research to bear on every aspect of Espronceda's life and writings.

17. Martinengo, Alessandro, 'Espronceda ante la leyenda fáustica', *Revista de Literatura*, XXIX (1966), 35-55. Concludes that Espronceda probably knew *Faust* through French translations.

18. Mazzei, Pilade, *La poesia di Espronceda*, Collana Critica (Florence, 1935). Interesting opinions. A particularly thorough review of possible sources.

19. Pattison, Walter T., 'On Espronceda's Personality', *Publications of the Modern Language Association of America*, LXI (1946), 1126-45. Studies Espronceda's development as a poet and puts forward an explanation for the pessimism of the later works.

20. Peers, E. Allison, 'Light-Imagery in *El estudiante de Salamanca*', *Hispanic Review*, IX (1941), 199-209. A perceptive article which increases appreciation of the text.

21. Pemán, José María, *Espronceda*, Nombres que son historia, I (Madrid, 1966). A readable biography, though some of its statements should be checked against the latest findings of Marrast.

22. Pujals, Esteban, *Espronceda y Lord Byron*, Anejos de *Revista de Literatura*, VII, 2nd edition (enlarged) (Madrid, 1972). A study in depth of the similarities and differences between the two writers.

23. Rodríguez-Solís, Enrique, *Espronceda. Su tiempo, su vida y sus obras. Ensayo histórico-biográfico* (Madrid: Imp. de Fernando Cao y Domingo de Val, 1883). 2nd edition, 1884; 3rd edition, 1889. A valuable early

biography and criticism.

24. Salinas, Pedro, 'Espronceda. La rebelión contra la realidad', in *Ensayos de literatura hispánica del 'Cantar de mio Cid' a García Lorca*, Ensayistas hispánicos, 2nd edition (Madrid, 1961), pp.259-67. Helpful for reaching an understanding of Don Félix.

25. Torre Pintueles, Elías, '¿Un antecedente de *El estudiante de Salamanca*?', in *Tres estudios en torno a García de Villalta* (Madrid: Insula, 1965), pp.117-30.

26. Ynduráin, Domingo, *Análisis formal de la poesía de Espronceda*, Persiles, 43 (Madrid, 1971). The preface is by Rafael Lapesa. Pp. 169-398 give an exhaustive commentary on the language used in *El estudiante de Salamanca*, in particular on the adjectives and on the general effects obtained in the poem.

WORKS FOR BACKGROUND READING OR CONSULTATION

On the *Danse Macabre*:

27. Clark, James M., *The Dance of Death in the Middle Ages and the Renaissance*, Glasgow University Publications, 86 (Glasgow, 1950).

On Spanish refugees in England during Espronceda's time:

28. Llorens [Castillo], Vicente, *Liberales y románticos. Una emigración española en Inglaterra (1823-1834)*, España y españoles, 2nd edition (Madrid, 1968). The only study in book form.

On Romanticism:

29. Praz, Mario, *The Romantic Agony*, translated by Angus Davidson, 2nd edition (enlarged) (London: Oxford University Press, 1951). There are many works on Romanticism, but Praz concentrates on aspects of the movement which are especially important for *El estudiante de Salamanca*, such as the Byronic hero, and the Romantic love of horror.

30. Shaw, Donald L., 'Spain: Romántico – Romanticismo – Romancesco – Romanesco – Romancista – Románico', in *'Romantic' and its Cognates: The European History of a Word*, ed. Hans Eichner (Manchester: Univ. Press, 1972), pp.341-71. An admirably concise and stimulating survey.

On versification:

31. Dreps, Joseph A., 'Was José de Espronceda an Innovator in Metrics?', *Philological Quarterly*, XVIII (1939), 35-51.

32. Navarro Tomás, T., *Métrica española. Reseña histórica y descriptiva*, 3rd edition (enlarged) (Madrid: Ediciones Guadarrama, 1972). A splendidly clear and easily consulted manual.